BETTY FOSTER'S DRESSMAKING BOOK

Macdonald

Editorial manager
Chester Fisher
Series Editor
Jim Miles
Editor
Linda Sonntag
Designer
Peter Benoist
Production
Penny Kitchenham

© Macdonald Educational Ltd 1979
Text © Betty Foster 1979
© *After Noon Plus* Thames Television 1979

Published in association with
Thames Television's programme
After Noon Plus edited by Catherine
Freeman

First published 1979
Macdonald Educational Ltd
Holywell House
Worship Street
London EC2A 2EN

Printed and bound by
Purnell & Sons Ltd
Paulton

ISBN 0 356 06319 4 (paperback edition)
ISBN 0 356 06320 8 (cased edition)

Contents

5 **Introduction**

6 **You and your pattern**

14 **Fashion from a diagram**

15 Basic dress with long sleeves

16 Waistcoats and other tops

18 Skirts

20 Trousers

22 Blouses

24 Zip-fronted coat with hood

26 Tunic overdress and T-shirt

28 Shirt dress

30 Smock dress

32 Capes

34 Drop-sleeved jacket

36 Evening dress/nightdress

38 Mid-calf or long dress

40 Wrapover

42 Bikini and shorts

44 **Techniques**

58 **Information**

62 **Index**

63 **Credits**

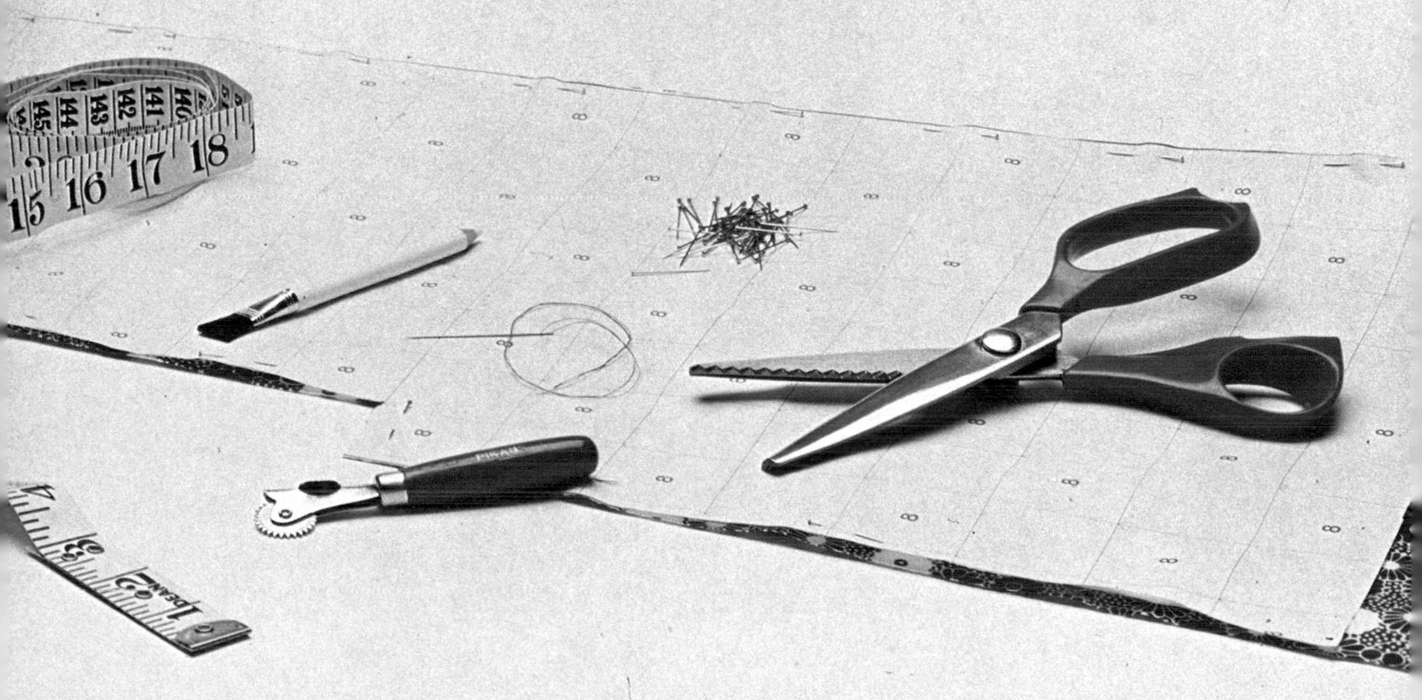

Introduction

Become a successful dressmaker and you will be able to create fashion for yourself and your family at an incredibly low cost.

The classical methods of sewing that you may have learned in school can often seem boring and fiddly. But sewing need no longer be a chore. The modern clothes manufacturer can't afford the time or money needed to make garments the traditional way, and so new easy methods have been devised to cut costs and corners. There's no reason why you shouldn't follow these at home, and this book tells you how. Just learn five basic techniques, and you'll be ready to sew.

The first basic of dressmaking is to get your pattern to fit, and this is clearly illustrated and explained in easy stages. Once you have plotted your Master Pattern, you will have understood the relationship of your body to the flat pieces of paper, and pattern alteration will no longer be a problem to you.

This book will be an invaluable aid in making up any patterns, but it also has its own pattern section which is versatile enough to provide you with a complete wardrobe. Designer Diagrams have been especially created to go with Designer Paper. You buy Designer Paper in the size you want to make (or in two sizes if your hips are bigger than your top, or vice versa!) and simply transcribe the diagrams onto the paper. There is no measuring involved in this, no mathematics, and certainly no drawing skill. Once you have seen how easy it is to sew the Betty Foster way, you will no doubt want to become your own designer and use the patterns in different combinations and with different materials for different occasions. You will find that all the pieces fit, and the world of fashion is at your fingertips.

Make a note of your measurements (including ease where necessary) on this Master Pattern.

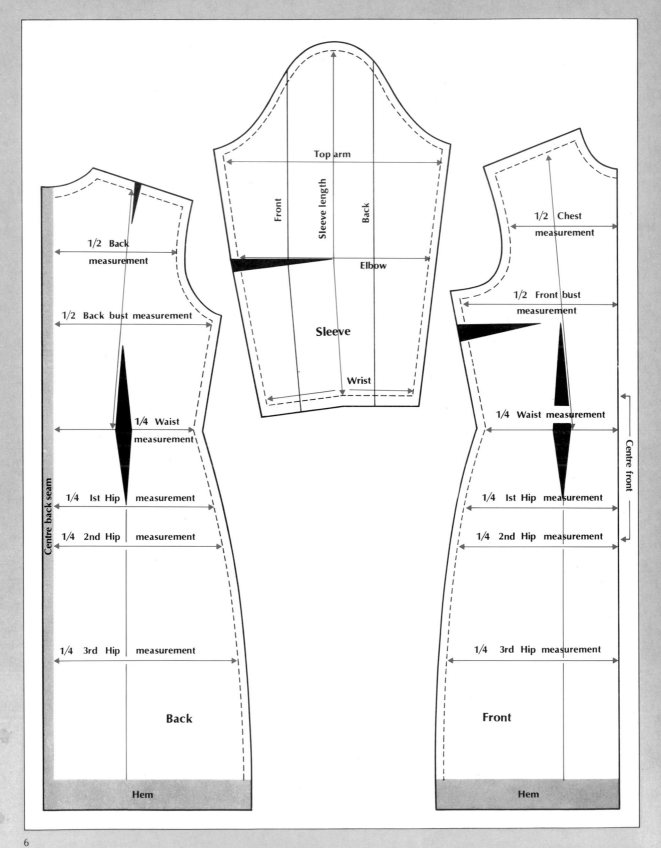

1/2 Back measurement

1/2 Back bust measurement

1/4 Waist measurement

1/4 1st Hip measurement

1/4 2nd Hip measurement

1/4 3rd Hip measurement

Centre back seam

Back

Hem

Top arm

Front

Sleeve length

Back

Elbow

Sleeve

Wrist

1/2 Chest measurement

1/2 Front bust measurement

1/4 Waist measurement

1/4 1st Hip measurement

1/4 2nd Hip measurement

1/4 3rd Hip measurement

Centre front

Front

Hem

You and your pattern

The most important piece of equipment that the dressmaker will ever use is the pattern. Expensive fabric and brilliant sewing skills will not be of any use if you have failed to understand the relationship between your figure and the flat pattern pieces, and to get the paper right before you start cutting it out.

For successful dressmaking, you will need a Master Pattern. Buy a simple fitted dress pattern in your size (see chart, p. 62) or copy the one on p. 15 onto your size Designer Paper. The pattern must comprise a one-piece front, one-piece back and long sleeves, which, when altered to your exact measurements, should fit you perfectly, providing a 'map' of your body and the basis for all the clothes you make for yourself. If you want to be sure of its fit, you could always make it up from an old sheet and practise your sewing techniques at the same time.

The Master Pattern is where the dress designer starts. The most important requirement when correcting your own Master Pattern is honesty: if the tape-measure tells you that your waist is two inches thicker than you thought, then believe it! Don't breathe in when you measure your waist and don't pull in your tummy muscles when you measure your hips. Stand normally, which may not be bolt upright, and wear the underclothes and shoes that you would wear with the finished garment. Take your measurements over a thin fitted dress or leotard so that you can clearly see your body's silhouette.

Decide whether you are working in inches or centimetres, then fill in your measurements in the spaces provided and *at each step* mark in the alterations you will have to make on your paper pattern, but at this stage *do not cut anything out.*

TAKING YOUR MEASUREMENTS: SHOULDER TO WAIST, BACK
From a point half way along your shoulder, take the tape-measure down to the waistline, marked with a ribbon, over the natural curve of your back.
Measurement =

Check with your pattern by measuring the line indicated from the shoulder to the waist. Make

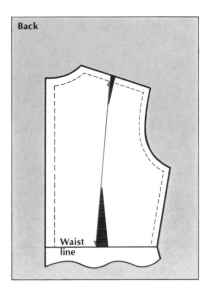

SHOULDER TO WAIST, FRONT
From the same point on the shoulder take the tapemeasure over and under the bust, down to the waistline.
Measurement =

no alterations until you have carefully looked at these measurements and your figure.

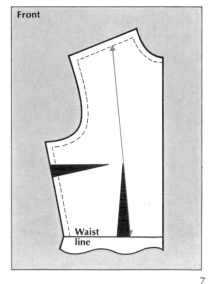

Choose a large flat surface to work on: if you haven't got a table big enough, a piece of hardboard will do just as well and can be easily stored under the bed.

The two measurements that you have just taken control the length of fabric required for the front and back bodice. The front should be *longer* than the back because of your bust shaping, and when the patterns are eventually joined together at the side seam, the difference in the length of these seams is the size of your side bust dart, which can vary from 1cm ($\frac{1}{2}$ inch) to 10cm (4 inches).

If you find the back is the same length, or even longer than the front, you must make adjustments to the back pattern before proceeding any further, to ensure that you retain a side bust dart.

When the back and front are the same length, cut a straight line down the pattern from A to B, and move the shoulder piece to the right, so that the cut is now 'V'-shaped. Take in the excess paper by folding a tapered tuck of 1-2cm ($\frac{1}{2}$-1 inch) at C. This will shorten the side seam and increase the shoulder dart (below).

When the back is longer than the front, indicating extra fullness in the shoulder area, make straight cuts in the pattern from A to B and C to D and spread to increase shoulder dart and lengthen back (below).

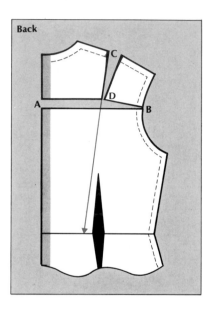

Alternatively, make the C to D cut in the neck rather than in the shoulder. Spread the pieces as indicated. This will produce an extra neck dart and lengthen the back. Both methods are ideal for round shoulders (below).

Make your corrections to lengthen or shorten the bodice now, on the line marked 'lengthen or shorten here'. It is unlikely that both back and front will need the same amount of adjustment. For instance, if you have a large bust, you will need more material to cover it, hence the front bodice must be lengthened, whereas your back measurement may be exactly the same as that on the pattern. Now you have adjusted the shoulders, if necessary, check your shoulder-to-waist measurement again on the pattern. Al-

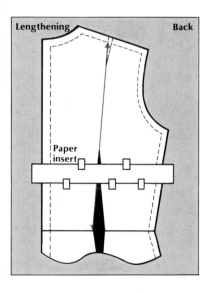

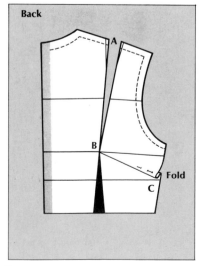

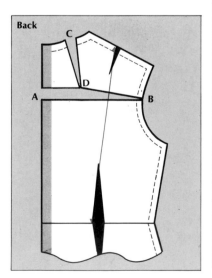

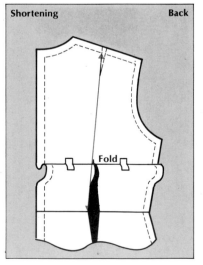

ways check your measurements within the stitching line. If you measure to the cutting line, you'll be making your garments too small.

Lengthen by cutting a strip of paper to the required width, cutting pattern on the line as marked and inserting the strip. Fix in place with sellotape.

Shorten by taking a tuck in the pattern and folding up the required amount as marked.

BUST

To all measurements taken around the body 5cm (2 inches) should be added for ease. This is very important, as even if you like your clothes to fit tightly you must allow room to breathe and move. 5cm (2 inches) may sound excessive, especially when it comes to measuring the waist, but measure any of your bought clothes and you will see that they are all bigger than you. This is the minimum amount of ease allowed.

Put the tapemeasure over the fullest part of your bust, note your measurement and add ease allowance. To make sure you have the correct fitting (remember that bust cup sizes vary, and so do the breadth of backs), pin a piece of tape from bustline to waistline under each arm at the side seams. Now measure the front and back halves of your body separately, adding 2.5cm (1 inch) ease to each measurement.

Bust + *ease* =
Front bust + *ease* =
Back bust + *ease* =

Check that front and back measurements add up to your all-round figure measurement!

Check with your pattern by measuring across line as shown, remembering to keep within the stitching lines. Mark your alterations on the pattern, but cut nothing out, as you have not yet checked the waist.

If your pattern piece is too big or too small, mark your alterations with a cross on the pattern as shown.

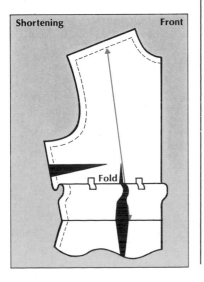

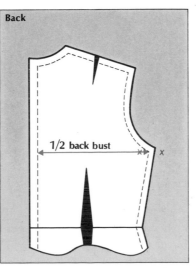

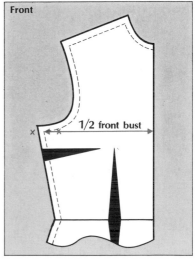

Never measure over darts: these will be taken out in the making up.

WAIST

Take this measurement, not too tightly, where your waist tape has settled (see photo on p. 7), and add an ease allowance of 5cm (2 inches).

Waist measurement + ease =

Check with your pattern. The waist measurement is normally distributed evenly between the front and back, so that each of the four lengths marked on the diagrams should represent about one quarter of the waist measure-

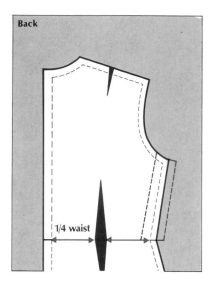

ment. *Don't* measure over the darts as they will be machined out to make the flat fabric take the shape of your figure. Correct at the side seam as shown. If the pattern is too small increase it accordingly and follow the blue line; if it is too big, follow the red. *Do not cut the paper yet.* Now you have corrected both bust and waist you can plot your final side seam by joining up your corrections with an even line. You are still not ready to start cutting out, as the hips are yet to come.

HIPS

Take three hip measurements and add 5cm (2 inches) ease to each. Check skirt length and add 5cm (2 inches) for hem.

1st hip + ease =
2nd hip + ease =

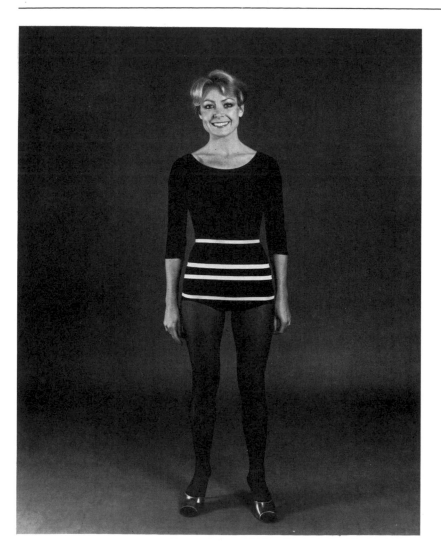

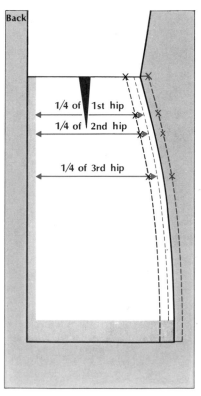

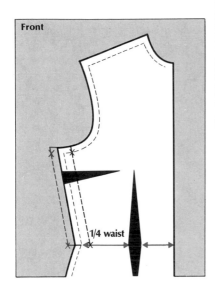

3rd hip + ease =
skirt length + hem =

Check with your pattern as for waist measurement. Mark your alterations as shown, making skirt lines flow smoothly into the waistline. Mark hem length.

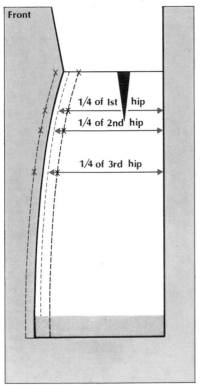

BUST DARTS

This is a crucial body fitting. Get it wrong, and your whole garment will be a disaster. First find out how high your bust is. Measure up from the waist to the point of the bust with a ruler.

Check with your pattern by measuring upwards from waistline as shown. Draw a line across your pattern at the height of the bust.

The size of the side bust dart is found by placing front and back bodice patterns side by side with waistlines level. The difference between A and B is the amount that will have to be taken in to make the two sides join up properly. This is your bust dart (C-D). Measure this distance *down* from the bustheight line and mark the dart as shown, correcting its position if necessary. (See diagram below.)

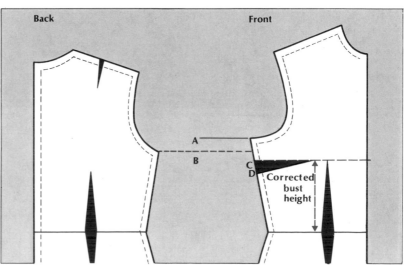

BACK, CHEST AND SHOULDERS

These measurements are all related; after all, you can't have broad shoulders without having a wide back. The chest measurement should be taken at the sleeve level, above where the bust begins to swell; the back measurement at the same level. The shoulder alteration will follow automatically.

Front + 2.5cm (1 inch) ease =
Back + 2.5cm (1 inch) ease =

Check with your pattern by measuring along line as shown.

Widen shoulders by making an 'L'-shaped cut down from centre of shoulder and out towards armhole. Pull the two pieces apart until correct measurement is achieved. Stick a piece of paper behind the cut and trim shoulder line.

Narrow shoulders by making the same 'L'-shaped cut and folding the pattern in until correct measurement is achieved. Secure with sellotape and level shoulder line by patching with paper from behind.

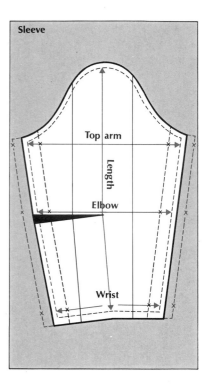

Sleeve

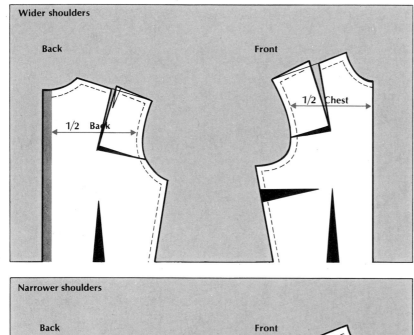

Wider shoulders

Back

1/2 Back

Front

1/2 Chest

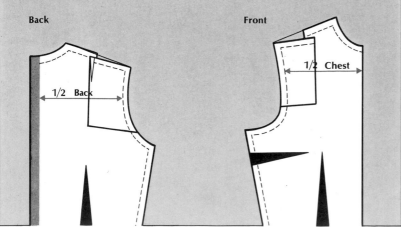

Narrower shoulders

Back

1/2 Back

Front

1/2 Chest

SLEEVES

Measure the length of your arm when bent. Add 3.5cm (1½ inches) ease round the arm where appropriate.

Arm length =
Top arm + ease =
Elbow + ease =
Wrist + ease =

Check with your pattern and adjust as shown, lengthening or shortening at the middle line as for bodice (p. 8).

Sleeve head and armhole
Once you have made your adjustments to the bodice and the sleeve, you will need to check that the sleeve head still fits into the armhole. Put back and front bodice pieces together at shoulder seam and measure length of sewing line with a piece of string as shown. Now measure round sewing line on sleeve head. The sleeve head will be bigger, be-

cause the sleeve needs to be eased into the armhole for a good fit, but if it is more than 5cm (2 inches) bigger, then decrease the size of the sleeve head sewing line by reducing either the sides or the head or both as shown in bright pink.

CUTTING OUT

Now the pattern is ready to be cut out.

Write in the measurements of this pattern in the diagram on p. 6 to keep a permanent record of yourself.

Your master pattern is the key to dress design and pattern adaptation, and once you have correctly mapped it out you are well on the way to sewing success.

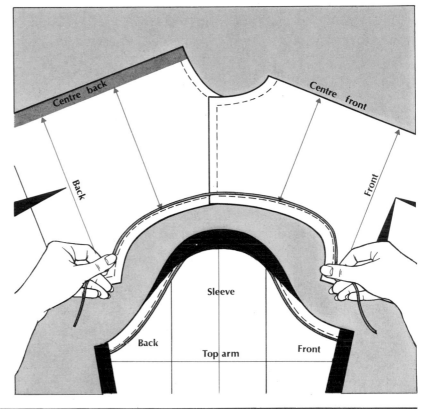

Fashion from a diagram

The Diagram Patterns illustrated in this book can be made up in countless variations. They have been designed to avoid critical fitting problems, and to allow the imaginative use of different fabrics to create your individual fashion wardrobe.

The principle of Diagram Patterns is very simple. The patterns are provided in this book on grids of 5mm squares. To make a full-sized pattern, all you do is transcribe the lines from the small squares onto the larger "squares" printed on Designer Paper. On each Diagram Pattern the range of recommended sizes is clearly stated. Check sizes at the back of the book.

Simply buy Designer Paper in the size you want to make. Prepare the paper by numbering the squares as they are numbered in the diagram, then copy the line from point to point. Transfer all the information from the diagram to the pattern pieces. Do not add turnings, as a seam allowance of 1.5cm ($\frac{5}{8}$ inch) has been included. Before pinning the paper on your fabric, check that the pieces fit together correctly. Note that facings are represented by a broken dotted red line.

Each garment has a chart recommending the width of fabric to buy. These widths have been carefully chosen because they allow you to simply fold the fabric in half lengthwise with the selvedge edges together. You then pin the pattern pieces into place correctly and cut out. (Any variation to this will be noted on the diagram.) Although this is not the most economical way of cutting out, it is the easiest way for the beginner.

The Diagram Patterns in this book have been especially designed to make the sewing as easy as possible. All the sewing techniques you will need are illustrated and explained on pp. 44-57. You will quickly see how often the same techniques are repeated in different garments, and particularly how few operations you need to learn to be able to make something to wear.

Chestlin
Bust

Waistlin

1st Hip
2nd Hi

3rd Hip

Waist
1st Hip
2nd Hi
3rd Hi

Basic dress with long sleeves

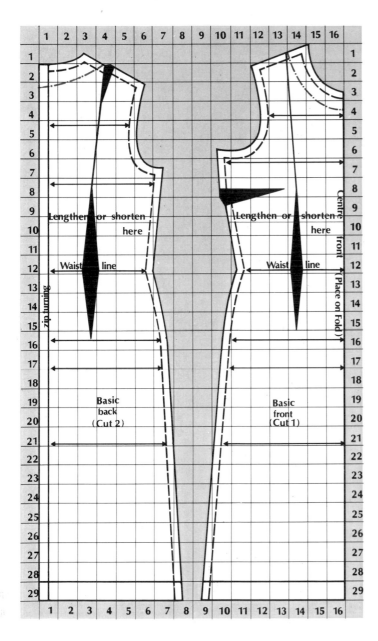

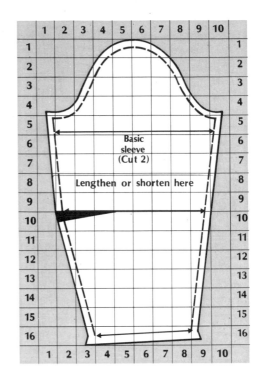

Press each operation as completed.
Neaten all raw edges.
Use matching thread throughout
and selected Vilene interfacing in
collars, cuffs and facings.

Order of making

1 Tack and machine all darts.

2 Tack and machine centre back
seam leaving zip opening.

3 Insert the zip.

4 Join shoulder seam of dress, also
shoulder seams of facings.

5 Attach facings to the neckline and
neaten back neck.

6 Join side seams.

7 Having machined sleeve dart, join
the sleeve seams. Leave sufficient
opening at wrist to get your hand
through.

8 Insert sleeve into armhole.

9 Adjust length of dress and sleeves
and hand sew into place.

10 Attach hook and eye at back
neck and press-studs to sleeve
openings.

Fabric required in recommended width and size range						
Size	10	12	14	16	18	20	22
m	3.00	3.10	3.20	3.30	4.00	4.00	4.00
yds	$3\frac{1}{4}$	$3\frac{3}{8}$	$3\frac{1}{2}$	$3\frac{1}{2}$	$4\frac{3}{8}$	$4\frac{3}{8}$	$4\frac{3}{8}$

Back zip: 50cm (20 inches).
Fabric: 90cm (36 inches) width.

Waistcoats and other tops

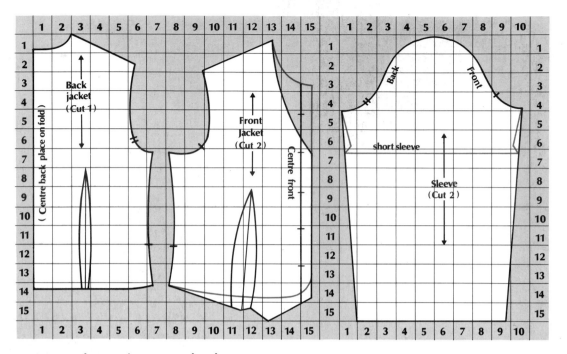

Press each operation as completed.
Neaten all raw edges.
Use matching thread throughout
and selected Vilene interfacing in
collars, cuffs and facings.

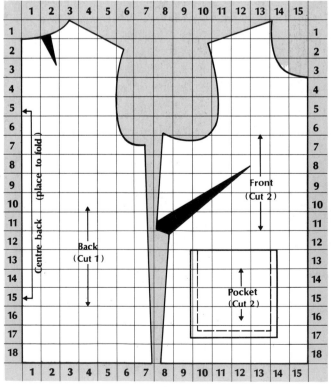

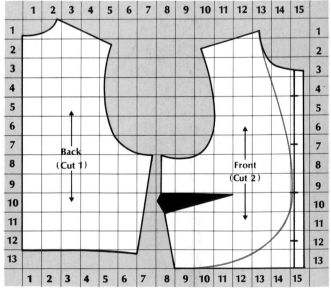

Cut lining exactly as main fabric pieces

Fashion from a diagram

WAISTCOAT

Fabric required in recommended width and size range							
Size	10	12	14	16	18	20	22
m	1.20	1.20	1.30	1.40	1.40	1.50	1.50
yds	$1\frac{3}{8}$	$1\frac{3}{8}$	$1\frac{3}{8}$	$1\frac{1}{2}$	$1\frac{1}{2}$	$1\frac{5}{8}$	$1\frac{5}{8}$

Short sleeve (optional) 0.50m ($\frac{1}{2}$ yd).
Fabric: 90cm (36 inches) width.
Lining same width.

BOLERO

Fabric required in recommended width and size range							
Size	10	12	14	16	18	20	22
m	1.10	1.10	1.15	1.20	1.20	1.25	1.25
yds	$1\frac{1}{4}$	$1\frac{1}{4}$	$1\frac{1}{4}$	$1\frac{3}{8}$	$1\frac{3}{8}$	$1\frac{3}{8}$	$1\frac{3}{8}$

For short sleeve add 0.50m ($\frac{1}{2}$ yd).
Fabric: 90cm (36 inches) width.
Lining same width.

Order of making

1 Machine darts in both the main fabric and lining.
2 Join shoulder seams in both main fabric and lining.
3 With right sides facing, machine the lining to the main fabric all round the edges *except the side seams*.
4 Push the fronts through the shoulders and out through one back side seam. Press the edges.
5 Join the side seams.
6 Position buttons and buttonholes.
NB: A set-in sleeve can be added and the waistcoat made up *unlined* with the edges bound. Otherwise the garment can be lined as on p. 48.

JACKET

Fabric required in recommended width and size range							
Size	10	12	14	16	18	20	22
m	1.45	1.50	1.55	1.55	1.60	1.65	1.70
yds	$1\frac{5}{8}$	$1\frac{5}{8}$	$1\frac{3}{4}$	$1\frac{3}{4}$	$1\frac{3}{4}$	$1\frac{7}{8}$	$1\frac{7}{8}$

For short sleeve add 0.50m ($\frac{1}{2}$ yd).
Fabric: 90cm (36 inches) plus lining same width.

Order of making

1 Prepare pockets and attach to jacket fronts.
2 Proceed exactly as for waistcoat.

Skirts

Press each operation as completed.
Neaten all raw edges.
Use matching thread throughout and selected Vilene interfacing in collars, cuffs and facings.

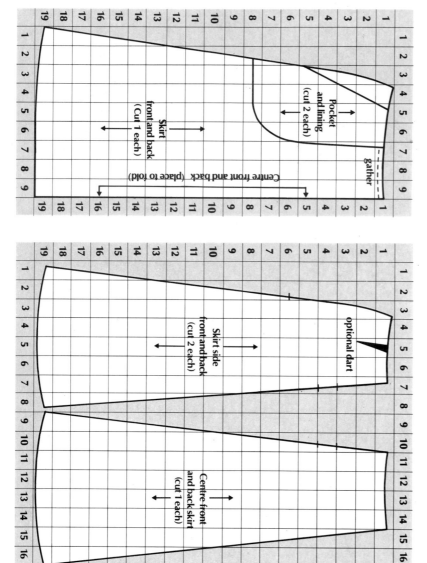

1

2

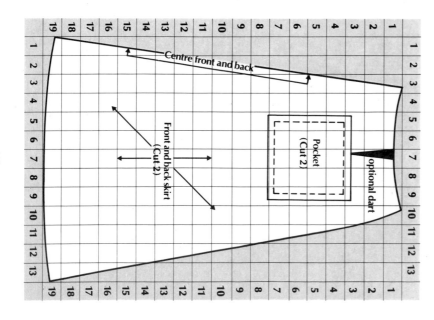

3

SKIRT 1

Fabric required in recommended width and size range							
Size	10	12	14	16	18	20	22
m	1.55	1.60	1.65	1.65	1.70	1.70	1.75
yds	$1\frac{3}{4}$	$1\frac{3}{4}$	$1\frac{3}{4}$	$1\frac{3}{4}$	$1\frac{7}{8}$	$1\frac{7}{8}$	$1\frac{7}{8}$

Fabric: 135cm (54 inches) or 150cm (60 inches) width.

SKIRT 2

Fabric required in recommended width and size range						
Size	10	12	14	16	18	20
m	1.55	1.60	1.65	1.65	1.70	1.70
yds	$1\frac{3}{4}$	$1\frac{3}{4}$	$1\frac{3}{4}$	$1\frac{3}{4}$	$1\frac{7}{8}$	$1\frac{7}{8}$

Pocket extra 0.35m ($\frac{3}{8}$ yd).
Fabric: 90cm (36 inches) width.

SKIRT 3

Fabric required in recommended width and size range							
Size	10	12	14	16	18	20	22
m	1.55	1.60	1.65	1.65	1.70	1.70	1.75
yds	$1\frac{3}{4}$	$1\frac{3}{4}$	$1\frac{3}{4}$	$1\frac{3}{4}$	$1\frac{7}{8}$	$1\frac{7}{8}$	$1\frac{7}{8}$

Fabric: 115cm (45 inches) width.

Order of making

1 Make your waistband to the required size.
2 Machine any darts or gathers where indicated.
3 Make pockets and attach them to skirt front.
4 Select position for zip opening, and join the appropriate seam leaving zip opening at the top.
5 Insert zip.
6 Join remaining skirt seams.
7 Attach waistband and add buttonhole or hook-and-eye fastening.
8 Adjust hem and sew into place.

3

1

2

Trousers

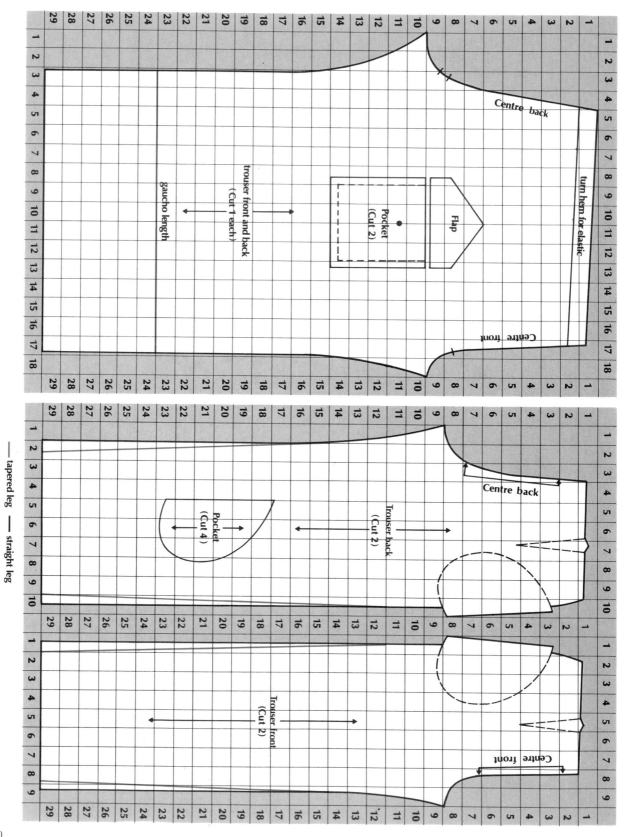

1

Centre back

turn hem for elastic

trouser front and back
(Cut 1 each)

gaucho length

Pocket
(Cut 2)

Flap

Centre front

2

— tapered leg — straight leg

Centre back

Trouser back
(Cut 2)

Pocket
(Cut 4)

Trouser front
(Cut 2)

Centre front

Fashion from a diagram

Press each operation as completed.
Neaten all raw edges.
Use matching thread throughout and selected Vilene interfacing in collars, cuffs and facings.

ONE-PIECE TROUSER

Fabric required in recommended width and size range						
Size	10	12	14	16	18	20
m	2.30	2.40	2.45	2.50	2.55	2.55
yds	$2\frac{1}{2}$	$2\frac{5}{8}$	$2\frac{3}{4}$	$2\frac{3}{4}$	$2\frac{3}{4}$	$2\frac{3}{4}$

Pocket (optional): 0.40m ($\frac{1}{2}$ yd).
Elastic for waist.
Fabric: 90cm (36 inches) or 115cm (45 inches) width.

Order of making
1 Prepare and attach pockets to each leg.
2 Join inside leg seams (press crease in each leg if required).
3 Join crutch seam.
4 Turn hem casing for elastic.
5 Insert elastic.
6 Adjust length and hem.

TWO-PIECE TROUSER

Fabric required in recommended width and size range							
Size	10	12	14	16	18	20	22
m	2.30	2.40	2.45	2.50	2.55	2.55	2.60
yds	$2\frac{1}{2}$	$2\frac{5}{8}$	$2\frac{5}{8}$	$2\frac{3}{4}$	$2\frac{3}{4}$	$2\frac{3}{4}$	$2\frac{7}{8}$

Zip: 15cm (6 inches). Waistband or curved petersham to fit.
Fabric: 115cm (45 inches) or 135cm (54 inches) width.

Order of making
1 Make waistband (as for skirts) or prepare curved petersham to fit.
2 Tack and machine darts.
3 Join pocket pieces to side seams.
4 Join side seams.
5 Join inside leg seams. Press crease in each leg, if required.
6 Join the crutch seam, leaving zip opening at either centre front or centre back.
7 Insert zip.
8 Attach waistband.
9 Adjust leg length and hem.

2

1

Blouses

SHIRT BLOUSE (SHORT SLEEVE)

Fabric required in recommended width and size range							
Size	10	12	14	16	18	20	22
m	2.25	2.30	2.35	2.40	2.45	2.45	2.50
yds	$2\frac{1}{2}$	$2\frac{1}{2}$	$2\frac{5}{8}$	$2\frac{5}{8}$	$2\frac{3}{4}$	$2\frac{3}{4}$	$2\frac{7}{8}$

4 buttons.
Fabric: 90cm (36 inches) or 115cm (45 inches) width.

Order of making
1 Prepare and make the collar.
2 Join shoulder seams of the blouse. Join shoulder seams of the facings.
3 Starting from the centre back, attach collar to neckline.
4 Join the facings to the blouse.
5 Set the sleeves into the armholes, *before* joining sleeve seams or side seams.
6 Join sleeve seams and side seams in one operation.
7 Try on and position buttons and buttonholes.
8 Machine hem as required.

RAGLAN BLOUSE (LONG SLEEVE)

Fabric required in recommended width and size range							
Size	10	12	14	16	18	20	22
m	2.90	3.00	3.10	3.10	3.15	3.15	3.20
yds	$3\frac{1}{8}$	$3\frac{1}{4}$	$3\frac{3}{8}$	$3\frac{3}{8}$	$3\frac{1}{2}$	$3\frac{1}{2}$	$3\frac{1}{2}$

Fabric: 90cm (36 inches) or 115cm (45 inches) width.

Order of making
1 Machine the darts in the head of the sleeves.
2 Join the centre front body seam leaving opening at the top to allow head to go through.
3 Join sleeves to front and back body.
4 Gather neck to required size.
5 Bind the neck, leaving long tie fastenings, or cut the wide tie and, treating it exactly the same as a *wide* binding, attach it to neckline in the same way that you attach a skirt waistband.
6 Make back opening in the sleeve.
7 Join side seams and sleeve seams in one operation.
8 Make cuffs to required size.
9 Gather or pleat the sleeve bottom to fit the cuff and attach cuffs.
10 Machine hem as required.

Fashion from a diagram

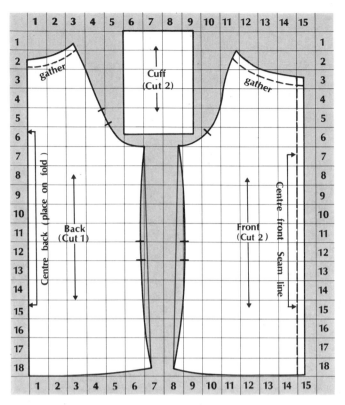

RAGLAN BLOUSE (LONG SLEEVE)

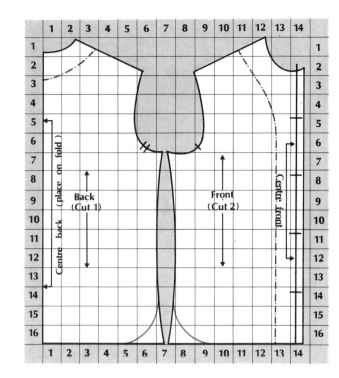

SHIRT BLOUSE (SHORT SLEEVE)

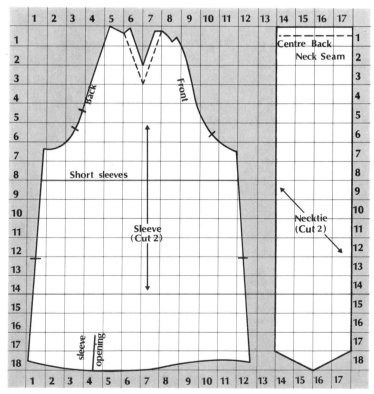

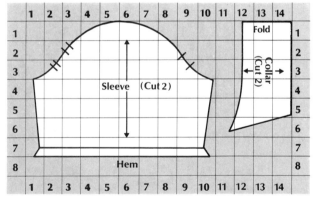

Press each operation as completed.
Neaten all raw edges.
Use matching thread throughout
and selected Vilene interfacing in
collars, cuffs and facings.

Zip-fronted coat with hood

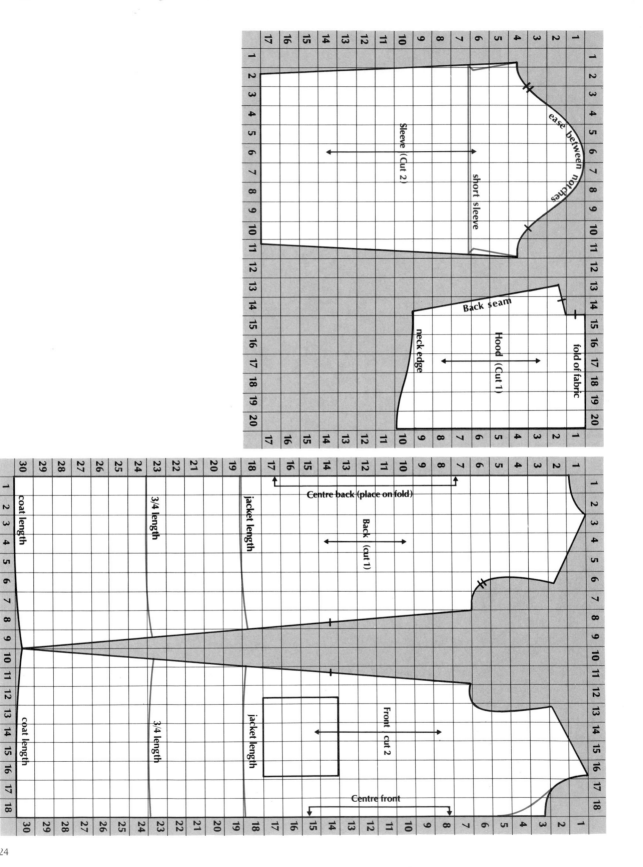

Sleeve (Cut 2)

short sleeve

ease between notches

Back seam

neck edge

Hood (Cut 1)

fold of fabric

Centre back (place on fold)

Back (cut 1)

jacket length

3/4 length

coat length

jacket length

3/4 length

coat length

Front cut 2

Centre front

Fashion from a diagram

**Press each operation as completed.
Neaten all raw edges.
Use matching thread throughout
and selected Vilene interfacing in
collars, cuffs and facings.**

Fabric required in recommended width and size range						
Size	10	12	14	16	18	20	22
m	3.40	3.50	3.55	3.65	3.70	3.75	3.80
yds	$3\frac{3}{4}$	$3\frac{7}{8}$	$3\frac{7}{8}$	4	4	4	$4\frac{1}{4}$

Braid to bind edges and open-ended zip.
Fabric: 135cm (54 inches) or 150cm
(60 inches) width.

Order of making

1 Make the hood. (A) Machine back
seam. (B) With right sides facing
bring the top fold edge down to the
back seam and stitch across the
opening.

2 Prepare pockets and attach to
coat fronts.

3 Join shoulder seams and side
seams.

4 Commencing at the centre back
neck, join the hood to the neckline.
Neaten the seam.

5 Join the sleeve seams.

6 Set the sleeves into the armholes.

7 Adjust length of coat and sleeves.
Hem as required.

8 Commencing at the bottom hem,
bind all round the coat including the
hood. Finish at the opposite bottom
front.

9 Insert open-ended zip to the
centre front, taking it well up to the
neckline.

NB: This coat can be made as a short
jacket or three-quarter coat.

Tunic overdress

Press each operation as completed.
Neaten all raw edges.
Use matching thread throughout
and selected Vilene interfacing in
collars, cuffs and facings.

TUNIC OVERDRESS

Fabric required in recommended width and size range						
Size	10	12	14	16	18	20
m	2.55	2.60	2.65	2.75	2.80	2.85
yds	$2\frac{3}{4}$	$2\frac{3}{4}$	$2\frac{7}{8}$	3	3	$3\frac{1}{8}$
Fabric: 135cm (54 inches) or 150cm (60 inches) width.						

TUNIC T-SHIRT

Fabric required in recommended width and size range						
Size	10	12	14	16	18	20
m	0.80	0.80	0.85	0.85	0.90	0.90
yds	$\frac{7}{8}$	$\frac{7}{8}$	1	1	1	1
Fabric: 150cm (60 inches) width.						

Order of making

1 Join centre back yoke seam,
leaving opening for neck zip.
2 Insert zip.
3 Join front and back of tunic skirt
to the front and back yokes.
4 Join shoulder seams of tunic and
of facings.
5 Join facings to tunic neckline.
6 Join side seams and underarm
seams in one operation. (Side splits
can be left as desired.)
7 Finish sleeve edge by hand-
hemming or machining.
8 Adjust length and hem as
required.

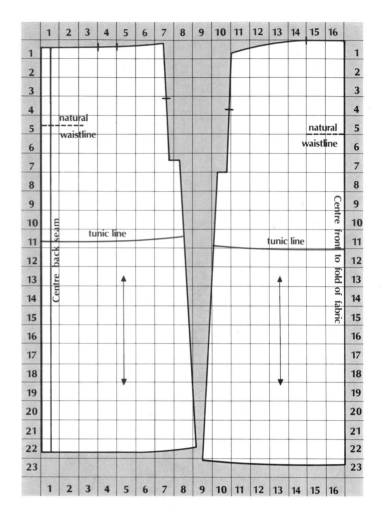

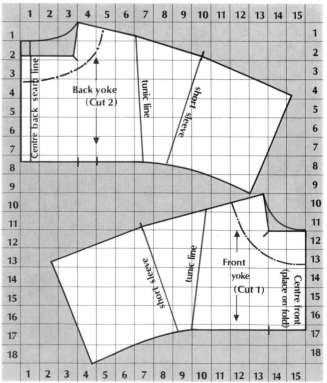

Shirt dress

Press each operation as completed.
Neaten all raw edges.
Use matching thread throughout
and selected Vilene interfacing in
collars, cuffs and facings.

Fabric required in recommended width and size range							
Size	10	12	14	16	18	20	22
m	3.70	3.80	3.90	4.00	4.10	4.10	4.20
yds	4	$4\frac{1}{8}$	$4\frac{1}{4}$	$4\frac{3}{8}$	$4\frac{1}{2}$	$4\frac{1}{2}$	$4\frac{5}{8}$

10 buttons.
Fabric: 115cm (45 inches) width.

Order of making

1 Prepare and make the collar and cuffs.
2 Gather back dress to fit back yoke, tack and machine into place.
3 Gather dress fronts to fit front yokes, tack and machine into place.
4 Fold back the front facing and join to the back facing.
5 Starting from the centre back neck, join the collar to the neckline.
6 Join the facing to the neckline and turn to the right side.
7 Join the side seams.
8 Make the back sleeve opening.
9 Join the sleeve seams and attach the cuffs.
10 Set the sleeves into the armholes.
11 Position button and buttonholes for both dress and cuffs.
12 Adjust hem and length as required.

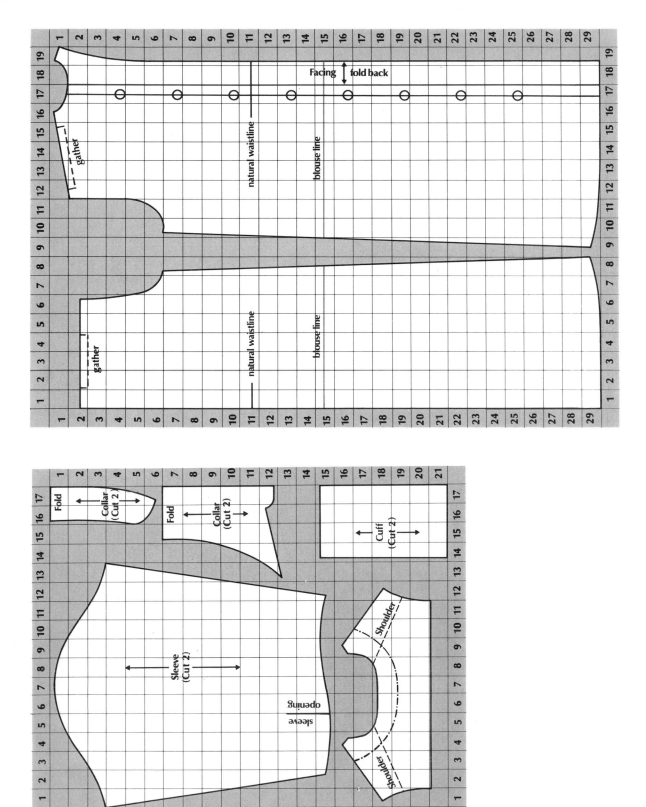

Smock dress

**Press each operation as completed.
Neaten all raw edges.
Use matching thread throughout
and selected Vilene interfacing in
collars, cuffs and facings.**

Size	10	12	14	16	18	20	22
m	4.30	4.35	4.50	4.60	4.70	4.70	4.75
yds	$4\frac{3}{4}$	$4\frac{3}{4}$	$4\frac{7}{8}$	5	5	5	$5\frac{1}{4}$

**Fabric required in recommended width
and size range for mid-calf length**

Short sleeve: 0.60m ($\frac{3}{4}$ yd) less fabric required.
3 buttons.
Fabric: 115cm (45 inches) or 135cm
(54 inches) width.

Order of making

1 Prepare and make the collar.
2 Join the shoulder seams of the
dress and the facings.
3 Starting from the centre back,
attach the collar to the neckline.
4 Attach the facings to the bodice.
5 Position the buttons and the
buttonholes and secure the
wrapover at the centre front.
6 Gather the front and back skirts
to fit the yoke.
7 Tack and machine the side seams.
8 Join the sleeve seams, gather the
sleeve head and set the sleeves into
the armholes.
9 Hem the sleeves and elasticate at
the wrist.
10 Adjust length and hem as
required.

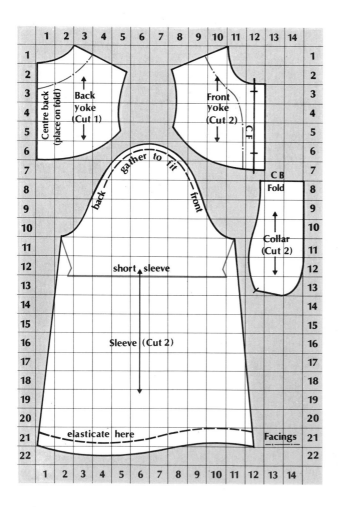

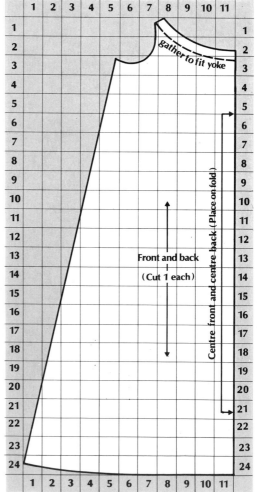

Capes

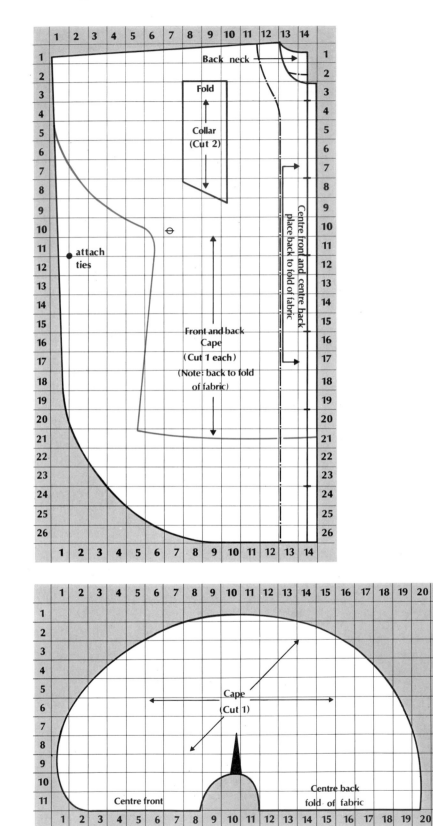

Press each operation as completed.
Neaten all raw edges.
Use matching thread throughout
and selected Vilene interfacing in
collars, cuffs and facings.

OUTDOOR CAPES

Fabric required in recommended width and size range						
Size		10	12	14	16	18
m	full length	3.10	3.20	3.25	3.35	3.45
yds		$3\frac{7}{8}$	$3\frac{1}{2}$	$3\frac{1}{2}$	$3\frac{5}{8}$	$3\frac{3}{4}$
m	$\frac{3}{4}$ length	2.50	2.60	2.65	2.70	2.75
yds		$2\frac{3}{4}$	$2\frac{7}{8}$	3	3	3
Buttons as required. Fabric: 135cm (54 inches) or 150cm (60 inches) width.						

Order of making

1 Join shoulder seams of main
pieces and shoulder seams of facing.
2 Prepare and make the collar.
3 Commencing at the centre back
neck, attach the collar to the
neckline.
4 Attach the facings to the main
garment.
5 Try on and position buttons and
buttonholes.
6 Check the length, then bind all
round the outer edges, starting at
the bottom centre back.
7 Attach ties or buttons and
buttonholes to the sides as
illustrated.

SHORT CAPE

Fabric required in recommended width and size range					
Size	10	12	14	16	18
m	0.80	0.85	0.85	0.90	0.90
yds	$\frac{7}{8}$	1	1	1	1
Fabric: 115cm (45 inches), 135cm (54 inches) or 150cm (60 inches) width.					

Order of making

1 Machine the shoulder darts.
2 Bind or neaten the outer edges.
3 Bind the neckline, leaving tie ends
to form a bow.

Drop-sleeved jacket

**Press each operation as completed.
Neaten all raw edges.
Use matching thread throughout
and selected Vilene interfacing in
collars, cuffs and facings.**

Fabric required in recommended width and size range							
Size		10	12	14	16	18	20
m	with long sleeve	3.60	3.75	3.85	3.95	4.00	4.00
yds		4	4	$4\frac{1}{8}$	$4\frac{1}{4}$	$4\frac{3}{8}$	$4\frac{3}{8}$
m	with short sleeve	2.90	3.05	3.15	3.20	3.25	3.25
yds		$3\frac{1}{8}$	$3\frac{1}{4}$	$3\frac{1}{2}$	$3\frac{1}{2}$	$3\frac{1}{2}$	$3\frac{1}{2}$
Fabric: 90cm (36 inches) or 115cm (45 inches) width.							

Order of making

1 Make the collar.
2 Prepare the pockets and attach to
jacket fronts.
3 Join shoulder seams of jacket and
of facings.
4 Commencing at the centre back
join the collar to the neck edge.
5 Attach the facings to the jacket.
6 Join the sleeves to the jacket.
7 Join the sleeve seams and the
side seams in one operation.
8 Try on and position buttons and
buttonholes or alternative fastening.
9 Adjust the length of the sleeves
and jacket and hem.

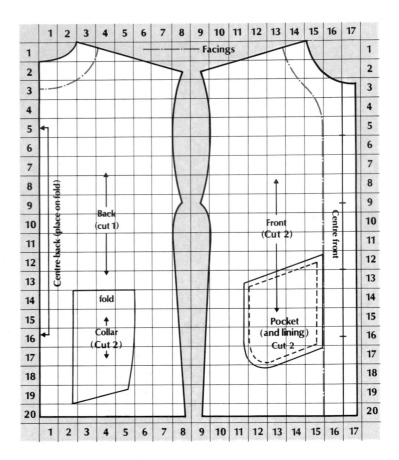

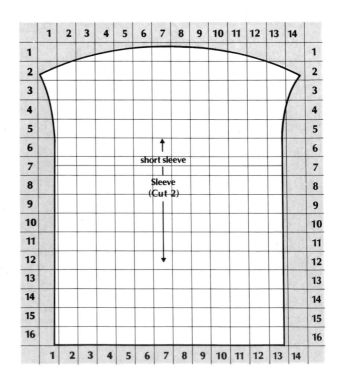

Evening dress/nightdress

Press each operation as completed.
Neaten all raw edges.
Use matching thread throughout and selected Vilene interfacing in collars, cuffs and facings.

Size	10	12	14	16	18	20	22
m	5.20	5.30	5.45	5.65	5.75	5.75	5.80
yds	$5\frac{3}{4}$	$5\frac{3}{4}$	6	6	$6\frac{1}{4}$	$6\frac{1}{4}$	$6\frac{1}{4}$

Fabric required in recommended width and size range

0.50m ($\frac{1}{2}$ yd) lining for bodice.
Fabric: 90cm (36 inches) or 115cm (45 inches) width.

Order of making

1 Machine darts in bodice front, also in the bodice lining.
2 Join centre front seam and side seams of the bodice and of the lining.
3 Make shoulder straps to required length and join to the top 'V' of the bodice and to the centre of each side-back.
4 With the right sides of the main fabric and the lining facing each other, machine all round the bodice edges *leaving the bottom open*.
5 Join the centre front seam of the skirt.
6 Join the centre back seam of the skirt leaving sufficient opening at the top to accommodate the zip.
7 Join the skirt side seams.
8 Join the skirt to the bodice.
9 Insert the zip at the back.
10 Adjust length and hem as required.
NB: This diagram can be used to make the pattern for a full length skirt.

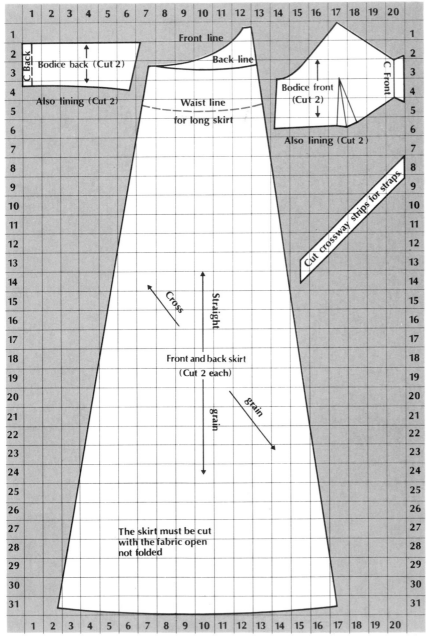

Long dress

**Press each operation as completed.
Neaten all raw edges.
Use matching thread throughout
and selected Vilene interfacing in
collars, cuffs and facings.**

Fabric required in recommended width and size range for mid-calf dress							
Size	10	12	14	16	18	20	22
m	2.55	2.60	2.70	2.75	2.80	2.80	2.85
yds	$2\frac{3}{4}$	$2\frac{7}{8}$	3	3	$3\frac{1}{8}$	$3\frac{1}{8}$	$3\frac{1}{8}$

0.70m ($\frac{3}{4}$ yd) lining for bodice and 50cm
(20 inches) zip.
Fabric: 115cm (45 inches) plus lining in
same width for bodice.

Order of making

1 Machine all darts in bodice of
main fabric and lining.
2 Join shoulder seams in main fabric
and lining.
3 With right sides facing, machine
lining to main fabric round the
neckline, armholes and down centre
back. Leave the bottom edges and
side seams open.
4 Turn right side out and press all
edges.
5 Join the side seams.
6 Join the skirt centre front seam
and skirt centre back seam, leaving
opening allowance for back zip.
7 Join skirt side seams.
8 Join the skirt to the bodice.
9 Insert the back zip.
10 Adjust length and hem as
required.

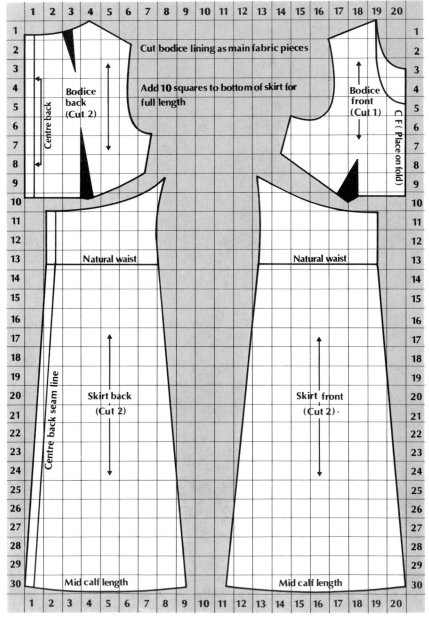

Wrapover

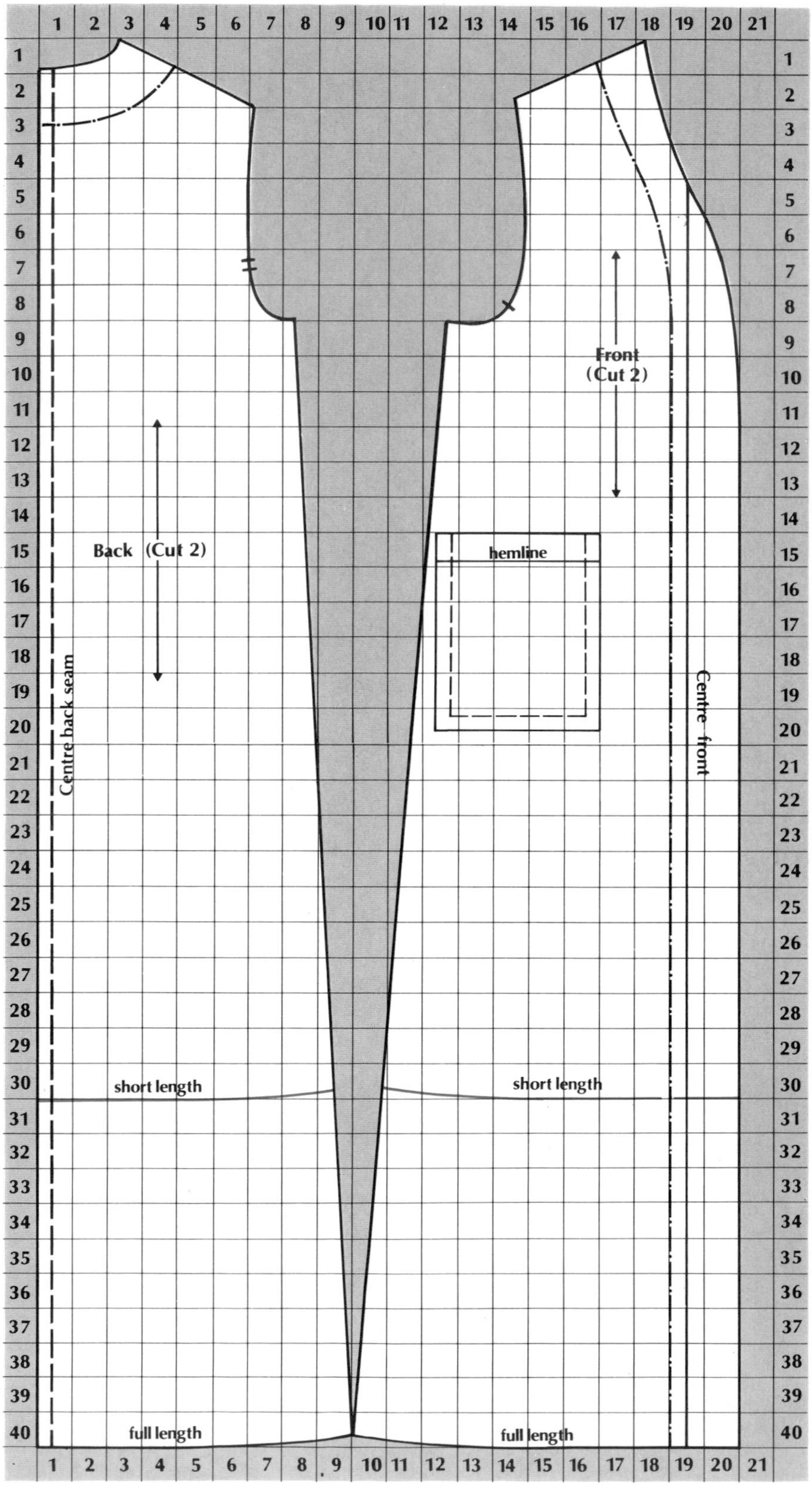

The diagram is a grid pattern (numbered 1-21 horizontally and 1-40 vertically) showing pattern pieces.

Labels on the diagram:
- Back (Cut 2)
- Centre back seam
- Front (Cut 2)
- Centre front
- hemline
- short length
- short length
- full length
- full length

Press each operation as completed.
Neaten all raw edges.
Use matching thread throughout
and selected Vilene interfacing in
collars, cuffs and facings.

Fabric required in recommended width and size range						
Size	10	12	14	16	18	20	22
m	5.00	5.20	5.25	5.35	5.45	5.50	5.55
yds	$5\frac{1}{2}$	$5\frac{3}{4}$	$5\frac{3}{4}$	$5\frac{7}{8}$	$5\frac{7}{8}$	6	6

Fabric: 115cm (45 inches) width.

Order of making

1 Prepare pockets and machine into position on front pieces.
2 Join shoulder seams of main garment and shoulder seams of facings.
3 Attach facings to main garment.
4 Set sleeves into armholes *before* joining the sleeve seams.
5 Join side seams and sleeve seams in one operation.
6 Adjust length and hem as required.
7 Make tie belt from a straight piece of fabric.

	1	2	3	4	5	6	7	8	9	10	11	12	13	14	
1															1
2															2
3															3
4															4
5					Sleeve	(cut 2)									5
6															6
7															7
8															8
9					straight sleeve line										9
10					flared sleeve line										10
	1	2	3	4	5	6	7	8	9	10	11	12	13	14	

Bikini and shorts

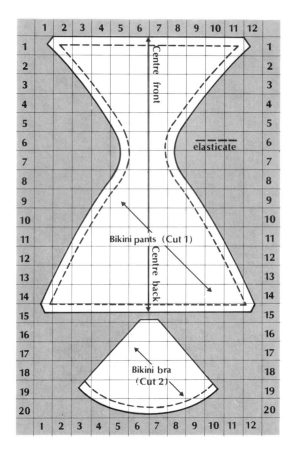

Cut lining as main fabric pieces

Press each operation as completed.
Neaten all raw edges.
Use matching thread throughout
and selected Vilene interfacing in
collars, cuffs and facings.

		Size	10	12	14	16	18	20
	Fabric required in recommended width and size range							
m	Bikini		0.80	0.85	0.90	0.90	0.90	0.95
yds			1	1	$1\frac{1}{4}$	$1\frac{1}{4}$	$1\frac{1}{4}$	$1\frac{1}{4}$
m	Shorts		0.80	0.85	0.90	0.90	0.90	0.95
yds			1	1	1	1	1	$1\frac{1}{4}$

Elastic for waistlines and cord for bikini.
Fabric: 90cm (36 inches) or 115cm
(45 inches) width.

Order of making

BIKINI PANTS

1 Turn the side edges and insert
elastic to give a close fit.
2 Turn top hem and thread cord
through the hem to form ties on
the hip.

BIKINI TOP

1 Cut main fabric and lining.
2 Sew cord to top of main fabric to
form halter tie neck.
3 With right sides facing, stitch
lining to main fabric leaving opening
at the bottom edges to allow cord to
be threaded through to tie at the
back.

SHORTS

1 Join the side seams.
2 Join inside leg seams.
3 Join crutch seam.
4 Turn top hem and insert elastic
to fit.
5 Adjust leg length and hem.

Techniques

Darts

When machining the dart, make sure your fabric lies quite flat, otherwise your dart will be twisted.

Contrary to what you might have been taught at school, there is no right and wrong way of dressmaking. There are several ways of doing everything successfully, and all are acceptable. Traditional methods, though reliable, are often difficult and fiddly, and such operations as putting in sleeves have been responsible for many people believing that they will never be able to sew.

To bypass these time-consuming operations, dress manufacturers have had to develop quick and easy techniques. There is no reason why the home dressmaker shouldn't take advantage of these. This book shows you various ways of performing each technique, so that you can decide for yourself which is the simplest.

The order of techniques follows the sequence of making garments, and once you have mastered the first five: darts, seams, zips, facings and hems, you will be ready to make your first clothes.

Darts are tapered tucks used to make the flat fabric take the shape of your body. Side bust darts and shoulder darts are marked on the pattern as illustrated below.

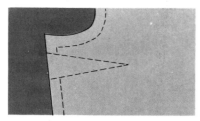

To save time, cut out the dart as shown below. Cut well inside stitching line but don't use this method on waist darts.

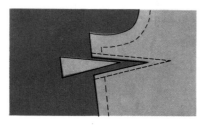

Other methods of marking the dart are with a tracing wheel and paper or with tailor tacks as below.

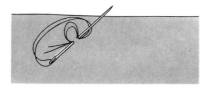

Cut the loops in the tacks, remove the pattern and cut the threads between the fabric.

Now fold the fabric wrong side outwards so that the dart is exactly in half, stitching lines together. Pin and tack.

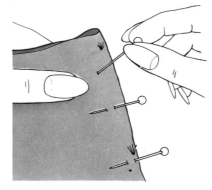

Machine the dart, beginning at the fabric edge and running off the fabric at the point. Secure at either end by reversing the machine or knotting.

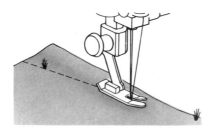

Waistdarts

Do not cut out waistdarts.

Waist darts are shown on the pattern as illustrated below.

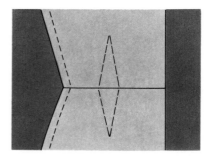

After cutting out the pattern, mark these darts with either a tracing wheel and paper or tailor tacks, as for side bust and shoulder darts. Fold in half with right sides together, pin, tack and machine from one end to the other as shown.

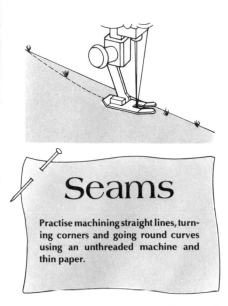

Seams

Practise machining straight lines, turning corners and going round curves using an unthreaded machine and thin paper.

The seam joins one piece of material to another.

The plain seam is most commonly used. Place the two pieces of material right sides together and sew parallel to the raw edge and 1.5cm ($\frac{5}{8}$ inch) within it unless otherwise stated.

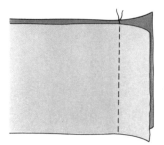

Many modern fabrics don't need finishing off at all, but if you have a fabric likely to fray, you will need to take precautions. Finish off your seams *before* you put the garment together, otherwise the job is endlessly fiddly. There are several ways of doing this other than oversewing the raw seam edge.

1 If your machine has a swing needle, then run a line of zig-zag stitching inside the raw edges.

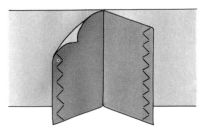

2 Failing this, turn over the raw edges once and machine.

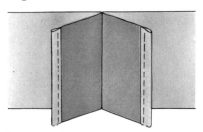

3 Cut each raw edge with pinking shears and machine a line of stitching just inside it.

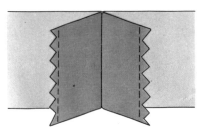

The French seam is ideal for sheer fabrics because it leaves no unfinished seam edges.

1 With wrong sides together stitch a narrow plain seam.

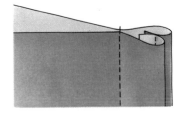

2 Reverse fabric and stitch second seam under raw edges of first.

Corners can be either inward or outward. Inward corners are found on square necklines; outward corners on cuffs, collars etc. As you machine round the corner, reinforce the seam with smaller stitches. Clip inward corner (below) to just outside stitching line to relieve strain when turned right way round.

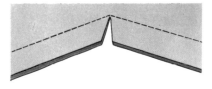

Trim outward corner (below) diagonally to remove excess fabric and ease turning to right side.

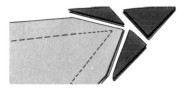

Seams on stretch fabric will be likely to break unless strengthened. Buy firm narrow tape and machine it into the seam.

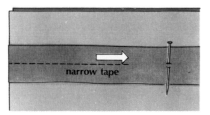
narrow tape

Techniques

Thick seams can be bulky and cause unsightly bulges. To avoid this, seams should be graded. In the diagram below, the seam involves two pieces of thick material, right sides together, and a piece of interfacing to firm or stiffen the area between them. After machining, cut the interfacing to 3mm ($\frac{1}{8}$ inch) above it, and the second layer about 6mm ($\frac{1}{4}$ inch) above that. When pressed flat from the right side, the seam should now lie smoothly.

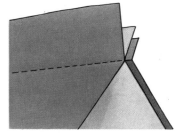

Curved seams can be inward, as on most necklines, or outward, as on rounded collars. Clip inward curves to relieve the strain when the material is reversed to the right side and notch the outward curves to remove the excess fabric.

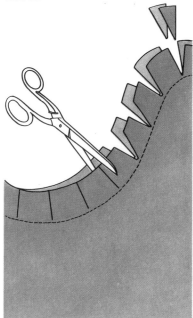

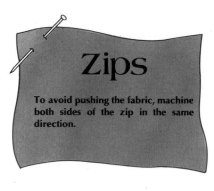

Zips

To avoid pushing the fabric, machine both sides of the zip in the same direction.

Zips often cause problems to the amateur dressmaker: in fact they can be put in in three easy stages.

1 For this operation it is essential to use the zipper foot. Place the zip under the fabric on the left-hand side. Position zipper foot accordingly. Start at bottom of zip and machine towards top.

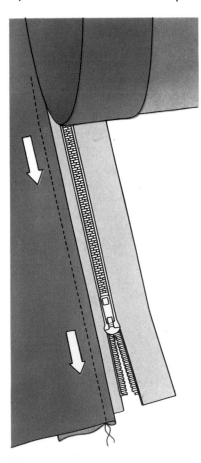

2 Bring the other side of the zip into position and tack or pin it into place.

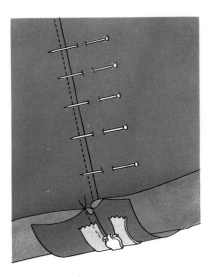

3 Move the zipper foot to the righthand position and begin where you started on the first machining. Machine across the bottom of the zip, turn and machine up righthand side of zip towards the top.

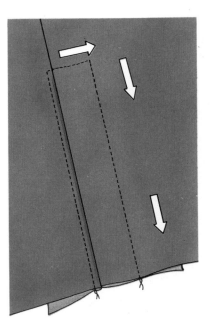

Facings

Try using matching lining for facings. It is less bulky and saves on expensive fabric.

Facings are a method of neatening raw edges at necklines, armholes and wrapover fastenings etc.

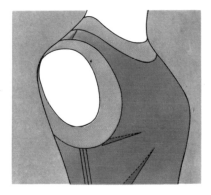

Facings are separate pieces on bought patterns, but shown on Designer Diagrams in this book by an alternating dash and dot line. If you are using Designer Diagrams, trace these pieces onto extra paper and cut your facings out from them.

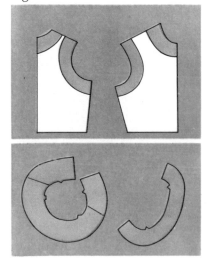

Sew the facings together as shown and neaten up the raw edges using one of the methods on p. 45.

Next stitch facings into the garment. For the neckline facing, make sure the centre front and back are matched, then machine the two pieces right sides together. Clip the inside curve (see p. 46). Turn to the right side and stitch through the facing and the seam to give a good neckline finish.

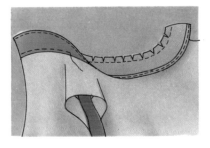

Follow the same procedure for the armhole facings, which are easier to deal with if sewn into the armhole before the side seams are machined.

To secure the facings, use one of the three methods below.

1 At a zip opening turn centre back edges of facing over top ends of zipper tape and hand sew in place. Add hook and eye if necessary to firm and neaten the opening.

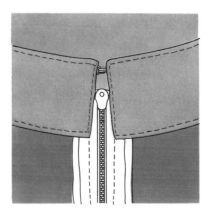

2 Hand tack the neckline and armhole facings to the seam allowance at the shoulder and side seams. Hold the material together and make four or five short stitches, 6mm ($\frac{1}{4}$ inch) or less, in one place through the two thicknesses.

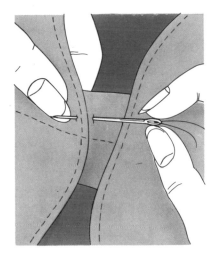

3 Machine tack facings where they will not show, such as under a collar or at a side seam. Working from the right side and keeping seamlines together, slowly stitch in the seam's groove for about 5cm (2 inches) from near the garment's edge. Secure threads by back-stitching or tying on the inside. (Shown below is the right side of the side seam under the arm.)

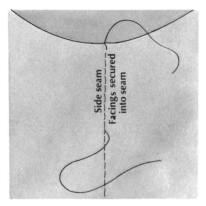

Techniques

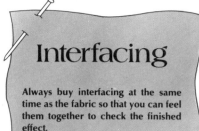

Interfacing

Always buy interfacing at the same time as the fabric so that you can feel them together to check the finished effect.

Interfacings, as the name implies, go between the main fabric and the facings. The most widely used are the non-woven variety, such as Vilene, which comes in a wide range to suit every type of material. Cut the interfacing to the same pattern as the facings, and use it too to stiffen collars and cuffs.

Iron-on interfacing can be very successful and is easy to handle, but always test it before applying it to your garment. Similar to this is a fusible webbing used for turning up hems without sewing.

Lining

Always use good quality lining and remember that a contrasting colour looks better than a bad match.

Lining is a professional and luxurious way of facing sleeveless garments and giving them a perfect finish. It is practically essential for its look and feel in jackets and waistcoats, where it can be as decorative as it is useful, but you might also like to line your dresses, at least in the bodice, and skirts.

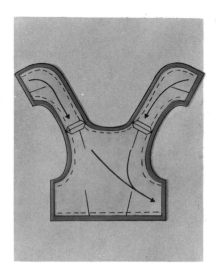

The above illustration shows a bolero in the process of being lined. Cut the lining exactly as the main fabric and then make it a bit smaller so that the stitching line will roll inwards by trimming off 3mm ($\frac{1}{8}$ inch) from all edges except the shoulder and side seams where it will be joined.

Prepare both fabric and lining by sewing the darts and stitching up the shoulder seams, working from the wrong side of each material as usual.

Now place lining and fabric together with lining uppermost, as above, making sure that right sides are together. Pin in place, then tack and machine all the way round the garment, *except for the side seams*.

Turn the bolero to the right side by pushing each front through the shoulder and then out through one of the side seams left open.

Sew the side seams, beginning on the lining 5cm (2 inches) below the armhole. Stitch down the lining and up the fabric until you can go no further. Finish off by hand.

Binding

Short of fabric? Binding with contrast material can solve the problem.

Binding can be a very simple and decorative way of finishing off raw edges and is especially useful when you haven't any fabric left over for facing neck and armholes.

Always cut binding on the cross of the fabric so that it will stretch, turn corners and lie flat when pressed.

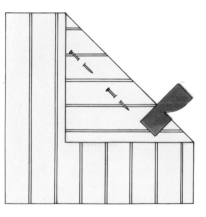

Cut binding approximately $3\frac{1}{2}$ times as wide as finished width required. Fold on the cross and mark cutting line with a measuring guide before doing so. Measuring guides can be bought from haberdashery departments or made at home from cardboard or paper to the shape shown in the diagram above. They are also very useful in hemming.

To join the strips of binding, put right sides together and stitch as shown. Now open out strip, press

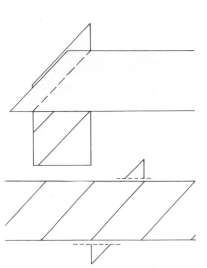

and trim off excess fabric to neaten.

To attach the binding, neaten one edge (see seam finishes, p. 45), and follow the method below.
1 With right sides together, stitch unneatened edge of binding to garment edge. The width of the seam should equal the finished binding width.

2 Turn binding over seam allowances to wrong side; pin in place from right side. Using a zipper foot, which can be attached to any machine, stitch in the ditch formed by the first stitching. If this is well done, the stitching will be invisible.

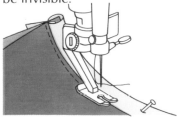

Hems

For easy hemming use a fusible iron-on webbing which will need no hand sewing. Available with instructions from haberdashers.

You will certainly need help to get the hem of your garment straight and even. Stand in a relaxed position and get your assistant to place pins *across* the fabric at the length desired at 10cm (4 inch) intervals, *measuring up from the floor.*

Take the garment off and tack a line between the pins with thread. This will be the line of the finished garment (not the hemline). Take the pins out as you go along. Now turn the hem up on the tacking line and pin it in place. Trim to an even amount, but don't leave a big hem on flared skirts as even a small hem will need little tucks to help it lie flat.

Hem by hand using a slip stitch or a herringbone stitch (below). Do not pull too tight.

Setting in sleeves

Always run a gathering thread around the top of the sleeve head to help you ease it into position.

Setting in sleeves has long been thought by students of dressmaking to be the most difficult operation of all, and indeed the traditional method (below) is very fiddly.

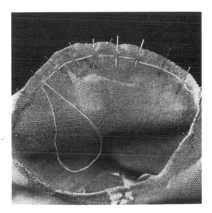

The conventional method of setting in sleeves is to first make up the sleeve, then run two lengths of gathering stitches (see p. 54) outside the sewing line on the

Techniques

sleeve head and within the seam allowance. The gathers are drawn up and the sleeve eased to fit the armhole on the bodice, which has also already been made up. The sleeve is then pinned, tacked and machined into position.

If you have mastered this method there is no need to change, but if not, there is a far simpler way of doing it, the way that the manufacturers use.

1 Machine together the shoulder seams of the garment, *but not the side seams*.

2 Gather the sleeve head, put a pin at either end and evenly distribute the gathers to fit the armhole.

3 Pin, tack and machine the sleeve to the armhole *on the flat*, before you sew up the seam of the sleeve.

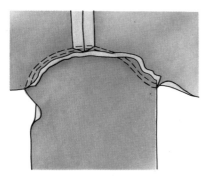

4 *In one operation* join up side seam and sleeve, starting at bottom of side seam.

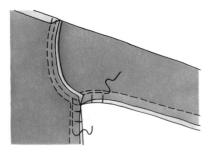

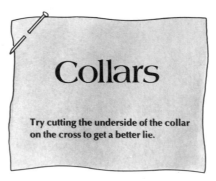

Collars

Try cutting the underside of the collar on the cross to get a better lie.

Although there are various ways of fitting on collars, all those introduced in this book have one thing in common: they are made up separately and then held in place between the main garment and the facing.

To make the collar, cut two collar pieces as instructed and place right sides together with interfacing (if any) on top. Machine the outer edges, leaving the neck edge open (1).

1

Cut the excess fabric away (see p. 45) and turn to the right side. Press (2).

2

Starting from the centre back (or front), pin, tack (3) and machine (4) the collar between the garment and the facing.

3

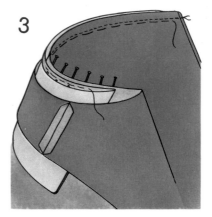

4

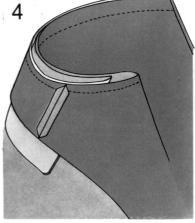

With this method you can make most types of collar except the traditional shirt collar.

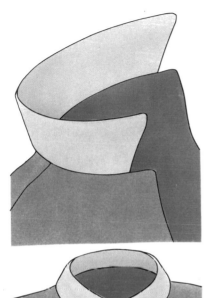

ends by back-stitching. Trim the top corners and make notches on the curved edges. Turn hem/facing to the wrong side and

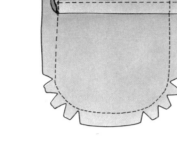

press. Press seam allowance to wrong side rolling the machine stitching to the underside so that it won't show when the pocket is attached to the garment.

To make a square, lined patch pocket, cut the lining to the same size as the fabric, then trim it by 3mm ($\frac{1}{8}$ inch) all round.

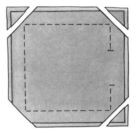

Machine the two together, right sides facing, all round, but leaving an opening so that the pocket can be turned to the right side. Trim corners.

Pockets

Pockets are one way of making a garment more decorative or useful without a pattern, and easy once you know how.

To make a curved, unlined patch pocket, cut round the shape indicated by your pattern and place right side up. Neaten the edge by turning under and machining. Now fold the top over towards you on the line indicated to form a hem/facing.

Starting at the top, stitch around the pocket on the seamline, not forgetting to secure both

Pin and tack the pocket to the garment as indicated on the pattern. Top-stitch into position.

Turn to the right side and hand-catch the opening. Attach to garment with top-stitching.

Techniques

In-seam pockets are concealed pockets most often used at side seams.

Before joining the side seams of your garment, cut out the pocket twice as indicated on the pattern. Place the pocket pieces in position on the garment as marked on the pattern, one on the front and one on the back of the garment with right sides facing (below). Where the pocket will open, sew each side to each side of the garment on the stitching line.

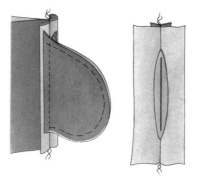

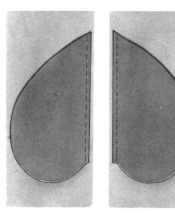

Flap the pocket pieces back and place garment right sides together. Sew on stitching line above and below pocket.

Now machine around the stitching line of the pocket, joining the two pieces together. Turn to the right side and secure neatly.

Sleeve openings

Always check that sleeve opening is at back of sleeve above the position of the little finger.

The position of the sleeve opening is always clearly indicated on the pattern. There are two types of opening.

The faced opening needs a strip of fabric cut 5cm (2 inches) wide and 2.5cm (1 inch) longer than the required opening.

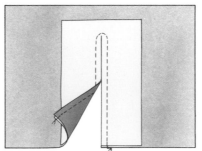

Place the strip on the sleeve as indicated on the pattern with the right sides facing. *Do not cut the slit.* Pin and tack into position and machine as shown. Now cut through the opening very carefully, taking care not to break the stitches. Turn facing to wrong side; tack and hem as shown.

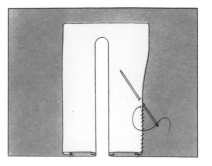

The wrap extension. Cut the sleeve opening (1) and a crossway strip twice as long as it and 2.5cm (1 inch) wide. Machine strip to opening with right sides facing (2).

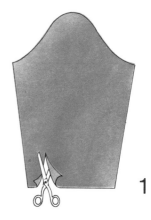

1

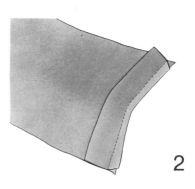

2

Turn fabric over to wrong side to form binding and sew by hand or machine into place.

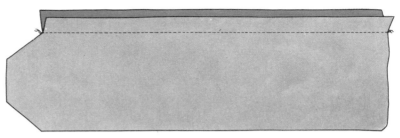

Tack and machine the two ends, leaving the sleeve seam open.

To attach cuff to sleeve, put right side of cuff against right side of sleeve. Turn back *wrong* side of cuff, as shown. Pin, tack and machine right side of cuff to right side of sleeve as shown.

The finished edge overlaps neatly. Add fastening.

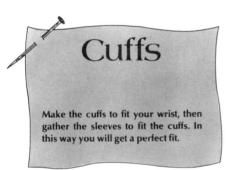

Cuffs

Make the cuffs to fit your wrist, then gather the sleeves to fit the cuffs. In this way you will get a perfect fit.

Cuffs can have either two square ends, or one square end and one pointed, which is buttoned above it.

Fold the cuffs, right sides together, and interface if necessary (see collars p. 50).

Gather or pleat sleeve bottom to fit cuff.

Finish by hand, slip-hemming, or by machine, catching the cuff to neaten the remaining inside edge. Complete with button and buttonhole (see p. 54).

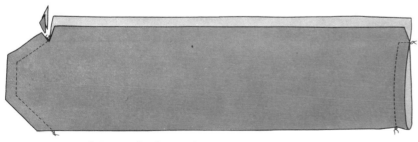

Clip points of buttonhole end. Turn cuff to the right side and make clip vertically as shown.

Techniques

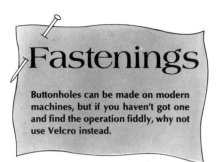

Fastenings

Buttonholes can be made on modern machines, but if you haven't got one and find the operation fiddly, why not use Velcro instead.

Hand buttonholes require a lot of practice, and even once you have mastered this very difficult operation, you will need a great deal of time and patience to apply it. If your sewing machine does not have a buttonholing device, then try to use another easier method of fastening.

BUTTONS

To position the buttons, wrap the buttonhole side of the garment over the button side, matching centre lines, and pin between buttonholes. Stick a pin straight through the buttonhole to mark the position of the button.

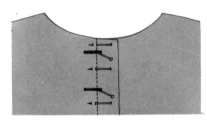

PRESS-STUDS

Mark the position of each side of the press-stud with pins as for buttons (above). Carefully sew each side of the press-stud into place.

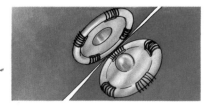

HOOKS AND EYES

When attaching hooks and eyes, always sew the hook side on first. Next put the eye over the hook and bring the fabric up underneath it. Now sew the hook into place, ensuring that the edges to be closed are exactly together or wrapped over correctly.

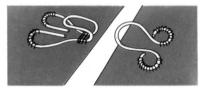

Gathering

Use shirring elastic to give that special gathered effect on sundresses and children's bathing suits.

To gather on a machine, adjust your machine to its longest stitching length and slacken top tension slightly. Machine on the required line.

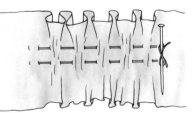

Machine two rows of stitching, anchoring the threads at one end securely with a pin. Gather gently by pulling the thread from the other end. Distribute the gathers evenly. It helps to mark off the sections. The best results will be obtained if twice the length material is gathered as is finally needed.

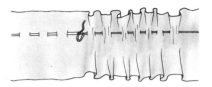

To gather by hand, secure the thread on the seam line at one end and use small, evenly spaced running stitches. Pull up the thread until the gathered piece is the required length. Do not machine gathers into place.

Place gathered strip of fabric between right sides of garment to be edged to form a frill. Machine along gathering line.

Trim excess fabric and reverse to the right side. Frills like this are very versatile on collars and cuffs as shown below.

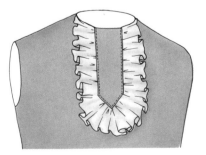

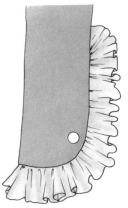

The circumference of the small circle (a) equals the length required, or half the length required if it's a long piece. To shape the flounce cut one edge straight and one edge curved as in the diagram.

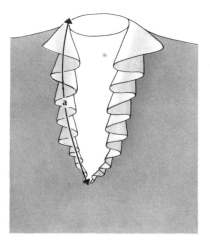

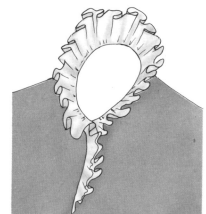

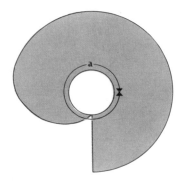

The frill above (like the neck frill in the top left-hand column) is a double edged frill. Cut a wide strip of fabric or lace twice as long as the frill length required and hem it at both edges. Gather in the middle for a neck frill or two thirds of the way across for a cuff frill and attach on the gathering line.

The flounced frill looks cool and elegant and hangs in soft folds. It is easy to make.

Cut a circle of fabric. Cut out a smaller circle in its centre.

Hem the outer edge of the flounce and attach down the neckline. This sort of flounce looks equally good on a cuff.

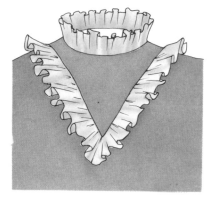

All these frills are made in the same way and attached between two layers of material or under a binding.

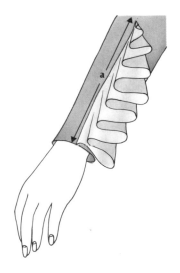

Techniques

Waistband

Make up the waistbands of skirts and trousers first. Cut the fabric to the waist size plus 10cm (4 inches) and 2½ times the required width.

If you don't want to make a fabric waistband, you will find that one of the neatest and easiest ways of finishing off the waistline is to use curved petersham. Note that the smaller curve will be uppermost and attached to the waist.

You will need the length of your waist size plus 10cm (4 inches). Machine the curved petersham to the *inside* top of skirt or trousers (1).

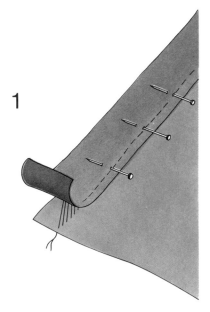

Turn the garment to the right side and neaten the fabric edge with paris binding. Insert two loops of paris binding at the side seams for hanging up (2).

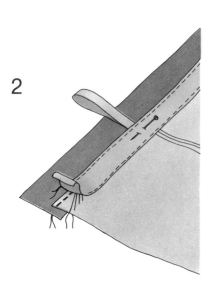

Turn the neatened petersham band to the inside and press the top edge (3).

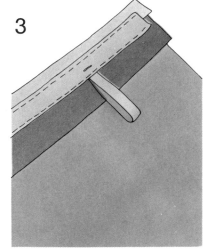

If you are making a fabric waistband you will need to stiffen it, otherwise it may lose its shape. Straight petersham is most commonly used and it is available in various widths. First cut your fabric waistband and petersham to your waist size plus 10cm (4

inches). Machine the waistband to the garment, then machine petersham to the seam (1).

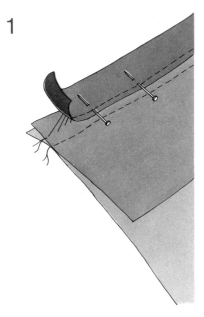

Neaten the remaining edge of the waistband, fold it over and finish by carefully machining from the right side (2).

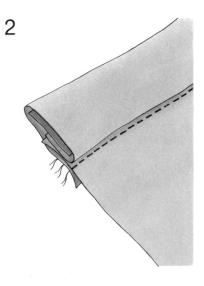

Various weights of interfacing can be used instead of petersham. The iron-on facings are particularly successful and should be cut to the waistband pattern.

2

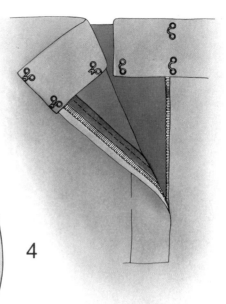

4

Position hooks and eyes carefully and sew firmly into place.

Elasticated waist

This is an easy way of avoiding making a waistband.

1

3

Attach the interfaced waistband to the garment (1). Leave sufficient wrap at each end to allow for the fastenings. Neaten these ends (2).

Finish the band by turning it over to the inside of the garment and hand sewing into place (3).

Position button and buttonhole fastening or attach hooks and eyes.

To elasticate a waistline you need to have sufficient fabric to fold over into a hem at the waist. Allow 5cm (2 inches) extra if not already allowed for on the pattern. Omit any waist darts which may be on the pattern.

Fold the hem over and machine into place, leaving an opening at the centre back to thread the elastic through. The elastic should be 5cm (2 inches) shorter than your waist size. Join the elastic and close the opening.

Information

Yards to metres

Yards	Metres	Yards	Metres
$\frac{1}{8}$	0.15	$5\frac{1}{8}$	4.70
$\frac{1}{4}$	0.25	$5\frac{1}{4}$	4.80
$\frac{3}{8}$	0.35	$5\frac{3}{8}$	4.95
$\frac{1}{2}$	0.50	$5\frac{1}{2}$	5.05
$\frac{5}{8}$	0.60	$5\frac{5}{8}$	5.15
$\frac{3}{4}$	0.70	$5\frac{3}{4}$	5.30
$\frac{7}{8}$	0.80	$5\frac{7}{8}$	5.40
1	0.95	6	5.50
$1\frac{1}{8}$	1.05	$6\frac{1}{8}$	5.60
$1\frac{1}{4}$	1.15	$6\frac{1}{4}$	5.75
$1\frac{3}{8}$	1.30	$6\frac{3}{8}$	5.85
$1\frac{1}{2}$	1.40	$6\frac{1}{2}$	5.95
$1\frac{5}{8}$	1.50	$6\frac{5}{8}$	6.10
$1\frac{3}{4}$	1.60	$6\frac{3}{4}$	6.20
$1\frac{7}{8}$	1.75	$6\frac{7}{8}$	6.30
2	1.85	7	6.40
$2\frac{1}{8}$	1.95	$7\frac{1}{8}$	6.55
$2\frac{1}{4}$	2.10	$7\frac{1}{4}$	6.65
$2\frac{3}{8}$	2.20	$7\frac{3}{8}$	6.75
$2\frac{1}{2}$	2.30	$7\frac{1}{2}$	6.90
$2\frac{5}{8}$	2.40	$7\frac{5}{8}$	7.00
$2\frac{3}{4}$	2.55	$7\frac{3}{4}$	7.10
$2\frac{7}{8}$	2.65	$7\frac{7}{8}$	7.20
3	2.75	8	7.35
$3\frac{1}{8}$	2.90	$8\frac{1}{8}$	7.45
$3\frac{1}{4}$	3.00	$8\frac{1}{4}$	7.55
$3\frac{3}{8}$	3.10	$8\frac{3}{8}$	7.70
$3\frac{1}{2}$	3.20	$8\frac{1}{2}$	7.80
$3\frac{5}{8}$	3.35	$8\frac{5}{8}$	7.90
$3\frac{3}{4}$	3.45	$8\frac{3}{4}$	8.00
$3\frac{7}{8}$	3.55	$8\frac{7}{8}$	8.15
4	3.70	9	8.25
$4\frac{1}{8}$	3.80	$9\frac{1}{8}$	8.35
$4\frac{1}{4}$	3.90	$9\frac{1}{4}$	8.50
$4\frac{3}{8}$	4.00	$9\frac{3}{8}$	8.60
$4\frac{1}{2}$	4.15	$9\frac{1}{2}$	8.70
$4\frac{5}{8}$	4.25	$9\frac{5}{8}$	8.80
$4\frac{3}{4}$	4.35	$9\frac{3}{4}$	8.95
$4\frac{7}{8}$	4.50	$9\frac{7}{8}$	9.05
5	4.60	10	9.15

Needles

Weight of fabric	Hand	Machine	Machine stitches to the inch
Very sheer	9	Fine 9	15-20 stitches to 1 inch
Sheer	9	Fine 11	12-15 stitches to 1 inch
Lightweight	8	Medium 14	12 stitches to 1 inch
	9	Fine 9-11	10 stitches to 1 inch
Medium	8	Medium 14	12 stitches to 1 inch
Medium heavy	6	Medium coarse 14-16	10 stitches to 1 inch
Heavy	4,5	Coarse 16-18	8-10 stitches to 1 inch

Zip lengths

4″	10cm	16″	40cm
5″	12cm	18″	45cm
6″	15cm	20″	50cm
7″	18cm	22″	55cm
8″	20cm	24″	60cm
9″	23cm	26″	65cm
10″	25cm	28″	70cm
11″	28cm	30″	75cm
12″	30cm	36″	90cm
14″	35cm		

48″	122cm
54″	335cm
58″/60″	150cm
72″	180cm

Fabric widths

35″/36″	90cm
39″	100cm
44″/45″	115cm

Vilene interfacing

All Vilene is washable and dry-cleanable and so it can be used with any fabric if the correct quality is used.

A40
Non-woven
Has no grain line
White
Lightweight
Cotton and rayon dresses
A50
Non-woven
Has no grain line
White
Medium weight

General purpose
S50
Non-woven
Has no grain line
Black
Medium weight
General purpose
A65
Non-woven
Has no grain line
White
Medium weight
Satins, tweeds and brocades
A80
Non-woven
Has no grain line
White
Heavyweight
For heavy satin and brocade
F2
Non-woven
Iron-on, has no grain line
White
Lightweight
For soft finish small areas only
F3
Non-woven
Iron-on, has no grain line
White
Lightweight
For crisp finish small areas only
O34
Non-woven
Has no grain line
White
Very lightweight
For voile, silk, taffeta
O32
Non-woven
Has no grain line
White
Lightweight
Light woollens and jersey
244
Non-woven
Terylene, no grain line
White
Lightweight
General-purpose synthetics
255
Non-woven
Terylene, no grain line

White
Medium weight
Coats
237
Non-woven
Has no grain line
Cream
Heavyweight
Pelmets, home furnishings

Note:
Vilene also produce a new interfacing 'Super-drape' for stretch fabrics. 'Wonaweb' is for hems without stitching and 'Fold-a-band' for waistbands.

Useful addresses

J & P Coats Ltd
39 Durnham Street
Glasgow G41 1BS
Manufacturers of threads and, under the *Pikaby* label, suppliers of a wide range of dressmaking aids.

J. V. Landers
21/22 Colebrooke Row
City Road
London N1
Specialists in permanent pleating of

all types, picot edging etc. For leaflet and price list send large stamped envelope.

Talon Textron
Treforest Industrial Estate
Pontypridd
Mid Glamorgan
This firm produces zips, including open-ended zips in non-standard sizes made to order. Details by post.

Fred Aldous Ltd
37 Lever Street
Manchester
M60 1UK
All handicraft materials.
Send 10p for catalogue.

Ellis and Farrier
5 Princes Street
Hanover Square
London W1R 8PH
Fancy beads and sequins. Colour catalogue £1 inc. p & p.

R. D. Franks Ltd
Kent House
Market Place
London W1
Workroom equipment and technical booksellers. Well worth a visit when next in London.

Designer Paper sizes

	METRIC							IMPERIAL							
		10	12	14	16	18	20	22		10	12	14	16	18	20	22
Bust cm		83	87	92	97	102	107	112	inch	$32\frac{1}{2}$	34	36	38	40	42	44
Waist cm		64	67	71	76	80	84	88	inch	24	25	$26\frac{1}{2}$	28	30	31	$33\frac{1}{2}$
Hip cm		88	92	97	102	109	112	120	inch	$34\frac{1}{2}$	36	38	40	42	44	$45\frac{1}{2}$

Useful sewing equipment

Part of the success in dressmaking is having the right tools for the job. These should include:

Tapemeasure
Linen or fibreglass are the best to buy because they do not stretch. You need one with the numbers clearly printed on either side. The tape-measure is often used on its side for measuring round curves, so the ones with a long brass end are not recommended.

Pins
Steel dressmaker's pins are essential. Cheap pins can mark the fabric.

Pin cushion
This saves money, and helps to keep your sewing area tidy. Magnetic pin boxes are also very successful.

Tailor's chalk
This can be bought in pencil form and in a variety of colours. It helps to transfer markings from pattern to fabric.

Dressmaker's scissors
Buying good scissors is essential. Make sure they are bent-handled, having a small handle for the thumb, and a large handle for the second and third fingers. Try the weight of the scissors in the shop to be sure that they are comfortable. If you are left-handed remember there are special scissors available for you. Take care of your scissors and do not lend them to anyone for cutting paper or other jobs around the house. Modern man-made fabrics blunt scissors fairly quickly so it is wise to check where you can get them resharpened.

Transparent ruler
This can be a great help when you are making patterns and checking measurements.

Flexible curve
You can buy it from most stationery departments. It looks like a length of coloured rubber, but is usually plastic with a metal core which allows it to bend round curves. Use it to draw up patterns, and to design necklines etc.

Seam ripper
A very economical item which speeds unpicking if you are unfortunate enought to make a mistake.

Thimble
Don't try to manage without one, as modern fabrics are very tough on your fingers.

Hand sewing needles
A good quality assorted pack could be your best buy. If you have difficulty threading needles there are very effective needle threaders in the shops.

Pressing equipment
An iron with a good temperature control is a vital piece of your dressmaking equipment. An ironing board with a separate sleeve board can be most useful. A linen damp-cloth might be needed for pressing, but remember that man-made fabrics can be ruined by too heavy pressing, and you should always test a piece of your material *before* going on to the main garment.

Hem gauge
A very useful metal or plastic gadget which helps to turn even hems on skirts and sleeves.

Sewing machine
Don't put your machine out of the way in between making garments. Get it out and practise. Use odd bits of fabric and keep a short zip handy to practise putting in zips. Unthread the machine and practise straight lines, curves and corners on thin paper.

Sewing thread
Always use a good brand of thread. Choose a colour slightly darker than your fabric, because it always sews in lighter than it appears on the spool. On your machine the top thread and the bottom thread should always be the same, except for decorative stitching when the 'bold' stitch thread is used in the needle.

Glossary

Armholes The opening in the garment where the arm comes out, and where the sleeves are set in.

Back stitch A reverse stitch on the machine used at the beginning and ending of the seams.

Balance lines The lines going across the basic pattern pieces which show how the back and front match together.

Bias Fabric, or binding, which is cut when the fabric is folded at right angles.

Binding A narrow strip of single or double fabric cut on the bias (often called on the cross), used to trim or neaten raw edges.

Casing A hem through which elastic or ribbon can be threaded.

Catch To attach one piece of fabric to another by hand sewing.

Clip Cutting a short distance into a seam. Used on curved seams, square corners etc.

Dart A short tapered fold or tuck which is sewn into a garment to give it shape.

Ease When one seam is joined to a slightly shorter seam without using gathers or pleats, the longer seam is gently 'eased' to fit the shorter seam.

Ease allowance determines the fit of the garment and is added to the body measurements to allow for movement.

Facings These are layers of fabric used to finish necklines, sleeveless garments, front and back openings etc.

Fashion ease is the fit of a garment decided by the dress designer to suit a particular style.

Grain The arrows on pattern pieces give the information required to follow the straight up-and-down or across weave of the fabric. These directions indicate the warp and weft of woven fabric, but the information must also be strictly followed for knitted fabrics. The bias or crossway direction can also be indicated in this way.

Hemline The position where the bottom of a garment is turned to the underside. Check that this line is an even distance from the floor all around the garment.

Interfacing A layer of carefully selected fabric, very often non-woven such as Vilene, which is placed between the garment and the facing.

Iron-on This is a term often used with interfacing, and it describes a specially treated fabric which is joined to another by using a warm iron.

Layering In a seam of several thicknesses each layer is trimmed to a different level to reduce the bulk and allow the seam to lie flat.

Layout The way that pattern pieces are placed on the fabric for cutting out.

Lining A fabric carefully chosen to complement the main fabric and which is used to completely cover the underside of the main fabric.

Markings The information on the pattern pieces which must be transferred to the fabric after cutting out.

Pinking A method of finishing seams with a pair of pinking shears, which cut a serrated edge. Not to be used with fabrics that fray easily.

Revers The part of a collar on a coat or blouse which folds back at the centre-front top.

Seam allowance The amount of fabric allowed for joining together sections of a garment.

Seam neatening The method used on cut edges to prevent the fabric from fraying.

Selvedge The finished edge of all woven fabrics running up and down the length. Now used to define the up and down edges of knitted fabrics.

Slash A straight cut in the fabric, such as is used for a sleeve opening.

Tailor's tacks The use of looped thread to transfer pattern information onto cut fabric.

Index

A

Armhole, fitting sleeve head into, 12-13

B

Basic dress with long sleeve, 15
Back bodice measurements, 7-9, 11, 12
Bikini, 42-3
Binding, 48-9
Bolero, 16-17
Bust:
    darts, 11, 44
    measurement, 9
Buttonholes, 53-4

C

Capes, evening and outdoor, 32-3
Chest measurement, 12
Coat, zip-fronted, with hood, 24-5
Collars, 50
    frills on, 54-5
Corners, seams round, 45
Cuffs, 53
    frills on, 54-5
Cutting out pattern, 13

D

Darts, 8, 9, 10, 44
    bust, 11
    waist, 10, 44
Designer Paper, 7, 14
Diagram Patterns, 14, 47
Dress:
    basic, with long sleeves, 15
    evening/night, 36-7
    long, 38-9
    over-, 26-7
    shirt-, 28-9
    smock, 30-31
Drop-sleeved jacket, 34-5

E

Ease allowance, 9, 10-11, 12
Evening dress, 36-7

F

Fabric Planner, 14
Facings, 47
Fastenings, 54
Flounced frill, 55
French seam, 45
Frills, 54-5
    flounced, 55
Front bodice measurements, 7-9, 11, 12

G

Gathering, 54-5

H

Hems, 10, 49
Hip measurements, 10-11
Hooks and eyes, 54

I

In-seam pockets, 52
Interfacing, 48

J

Jacket, 16-17
    drop-sleeved, 34-5

L

Lengthening bodice pattern, 8-9
Lining, 48
Long dress, 38-9

M

Master Pattern, 6, 7-13
Measurements, 7-12

N

Nightdress, 36-7

O

Overdress, tunic, 26-7

P

Pattern, making master, 7-13
Pockets, 51-2
Press-studs, 54

S

Seams, 45-6
Setting in sleeves, 49-50
Shirring elastic, 54
Shirt dress, 28-9
Shortening bodice pattern, 8-9
Shorts, 42-3
Shoulder measurement, 8, 12
Skirts, 18-19
    hip measurements for, 10-11
Sleeves:
    attaching cuff to, 53
    head and armhole, 12-13
    measurements, 12
    openings, 52
    setting in, 49-50
Smock dress, 30-31
Stretch fabric, seams on, 45

T

Tops, 16-17
Trousers, 20-21
T-shirt, tunic, 26-7
Tunic overdress, 26-7
Tunic T-shirt, 26-7

W

Waist measurement, 10
Waistbands, 56-7
Waistcoat, 16-17
Waistdarts, 44
Webbing, fusible iron-on, 49
Wrapover, 40-41

Z

Zipper foot, 46, 49
Zips, 46

Credits

Artwork

Ron Hayward Art Group
Mary Bridges

Photography

Jo Toriati
Paul Forrester (pp. 2, 3)

Cover design

Camron

Cover photograph

Clay Perry

Dressmaking Designer Paper

To make the garments illustrated in this book you will need Betty Foster's Dressmaking Designer Paper. The paper is available in seven sizes: 10, 12, 14, 16, 18, 20, 22, and can be obtained from all good stationers and haberdashers. In case of difficulty send the correct money plus 10p for postage and packing to:

Betty Foster (Fashion Sewing) Ltd
P.O. Box 28
Crewe
Cheshire

Each pack costs 59p and consists of three sheets of the specially designed grid paper. Please state clearly the number and size of packs you require and your name and address.